Nigel Coates | The City in Motion | *By Rick Poynor*

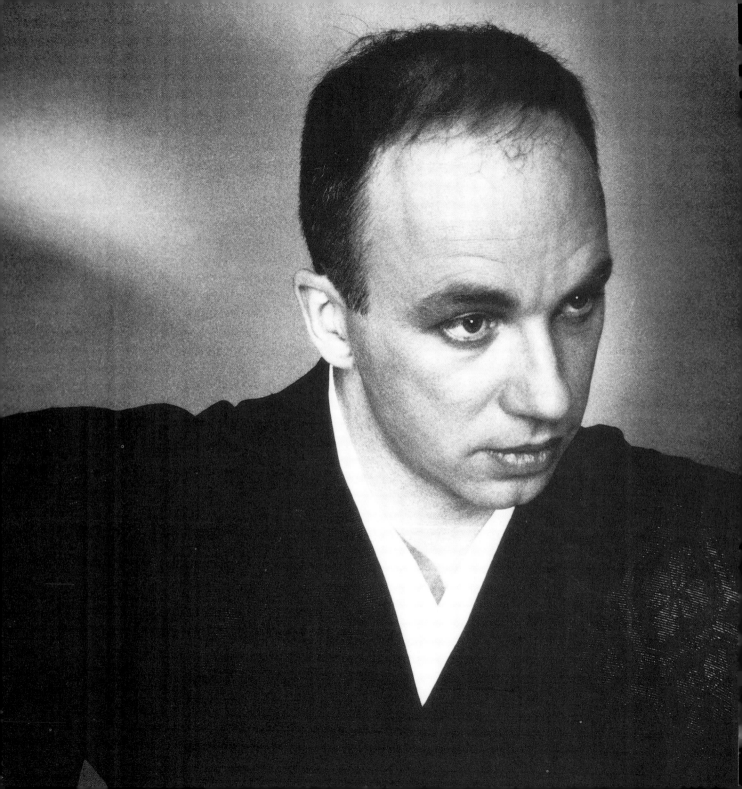

Nigel Coates | The City in Motion | *By Rick Poynor*

RIZZOLI
NEW YORK

First published in the United States of America in
1990 by Rizzoli International Publications Inc.,
300 Park Avenue South, New York, NY 10010

First published in Great Britain in 1989 by Fourth
Estate Ltd in conjunction with Blueprint magazine

ISBN 0-8478-1164-6
LC 89-62781

Designed by Stephen Coates
Edited by Paula Iley
Front cover photograph by Phil Sayer
Typeset by Offshoot Graphics Ltd
Colour reproduction by Precise Litho Ltd
Printed and bound by Pensord Press Ltd, Wales, UK

Acknowledgements
For the time they gave me and for the many
insights they shared I should like to thank Nigel
Coates, Doug Branson, Mark Prizeman, Carlos
Villanueva Brandt, Peter Fleissig, Robert Mull,
Catrina Beevor, Melanie Sainsbury, Christina
Norton, Alvin Boyarsky, Bernard Tschumi, Jenny
Lowe, Iwona Blazwick and Shi Yu Chen. My
gratitude, too, to Vicky Wilson, Hilary Young,
Deyan Sudjic and Paula Iley for their comments on
the manuscript; to Anne Brooks, Louisa Millar and
Jo Vernon for their patience in compiling material
for the book; and to Risa Katoh and Shinro Ohtake
for helping to make sense of Tokyo. *Rick Poynor*

Picture credits
Architectural Association pp. 29, 30, 32; Ed
Barber p. 83; Richard Bryant pp. 76, 77, 80, 82;
Alastair Hunter pp. 86–87, 88–89, 90; Peter
Fleissig pp. 8, 9, 38, 39; Edward Valentine Hames
pp. 43, 52–53, 54, 58, 62, back cover; Institute of
Contemporary Art, Boston p. 42; Institute of
Contemporary Arts, London p. 104; M. Massalini
and G. Trebbi p. 11; Cindy Palmano pp. 2, 106;
Sheila Rock p. 28; Frederick Rotkopf p. 103;
Superstudio p. 17; Bernard Tschumi p. 23;
Trustees of the Tate Gallery p. 34; Victoria and
Albert Museum prints and drawings collection
p.79, 81; Carlos Villanueva Brandt pp. 33, 41; Paul
Warchol pp. 51, 55, 56, 59, 60; Alan Williams
pp. 92, 93. Other material: Nigel Coates/Branson
Coates Architecture.

Contents

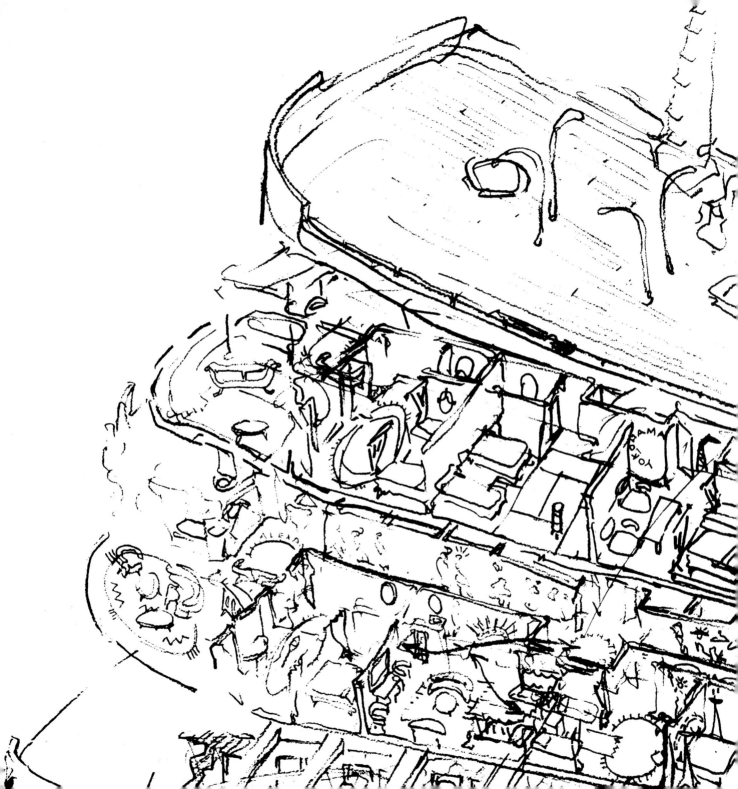

Introduction

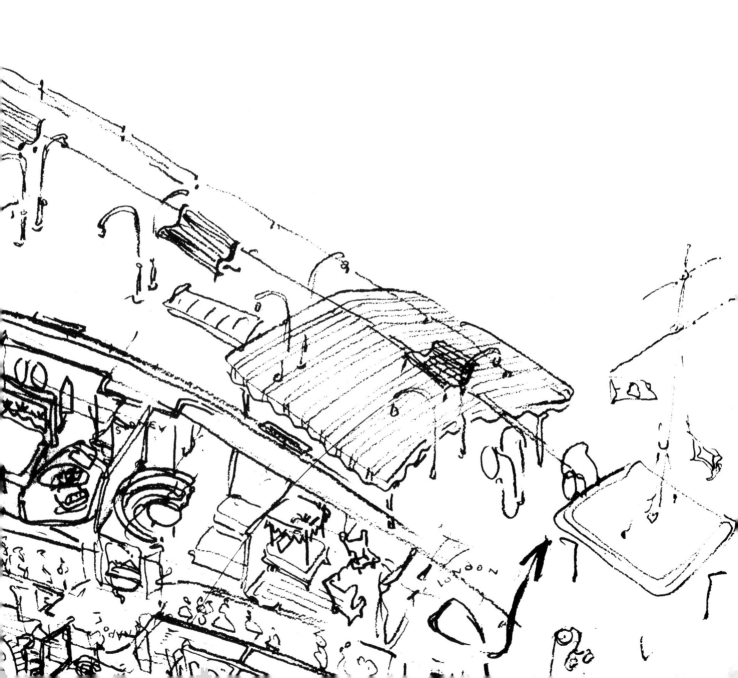

Of all the designers who came to fame in the 1980s, few have described a trajectory that more closely reflects the decade's obsession with design than Nigel Coates. In 1980, Coates was a tutor at the Architectural Association in London with not one built project, apart from the interior of his own flat, to his name. Like others of his generation of architects, he had graduated during the recessionary 1970s to discover that opportunities to build were few and far between. A life of teaching, theory and "paper architecture" seemed a lot more attractive than grubbing around for flat conversions or toiling in the offices of one of the bigger and duller practices.

By the end of the booming 1980s, however, Coates had a twenty-strong practice of his own, a partner, Doug Branson, and a string of completed projects to his name, the most extraordinary of which – Caffè Bongo, the Metropole restaurant, the Bohemia jazz club and L'Arca di Noè – were built not in Britain but Japan. When Coates said, "We're more an architectural airline than a conventional office" and dressed his staff in air crew uniforms for an office-opening party, it was with good reason.[1] He might not have been the only designer to export his talents to a Japanese market hungry for Western authenticity in the middle of the 1980s, but he was the only British architect who had to travel to Tokyo to convince his countrymen that his architectural visions amounted to anything more than a portfolio of fancy but unbuildable drawings. In the process of commenting on the culture he found there, he had produced some of the most remarkable and widely published interiors of the 1980s. As *Architectural Record* observed in 1987: "Though not well known outside fashionable London circles, the 38-year-old Englishman has succeeded in outshining his European colleagues by pinching the very nerve of Tokyo itself."[2]

For Coates, this association with "fashionable London" has proved to be a mixed blessing. In the 1980s, architecture and fashion have converged to an unprecedented degree, but this equation of "timeless" building and ephemeral clothing leaves many architects feeling uneasy. Coates, by contrast, has made no secret of the fact that he feels closer to fashion people than to fellow architects. His admiration for Vivienne Westwood, his projects for Katharine Hamnett and Jasper Conran and the regularity with which he appears, fashionably kitted out, in the pages of *Vogue, Tatler, Arena* or *The Face* suggest, to the more earnest end of the profession, an architect less preoccupied with matters of substance

8

Previous page, detail of Coates's drawing of the Otaru Marittimo hotel in Japan

The imagery of air travel is a constant theme of Branson Coates's work in Japan, as the team acknowledged when they dressed up in air crew uniforms for an office party. Back left, Doug Branson. Back right, Nigel Coates. Front left, Anne Brooks

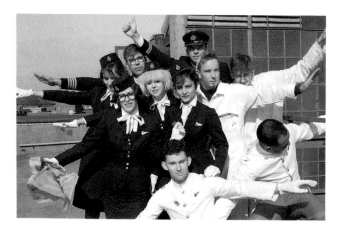

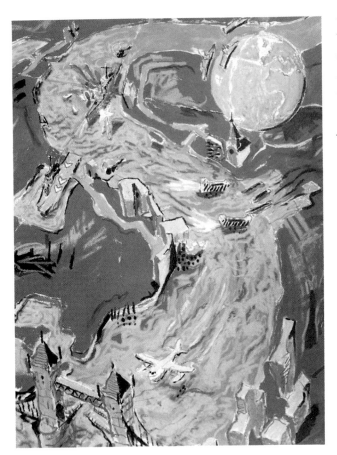

than with image. Even NATO (Narrative Architecture Today), the anarchic architecture group he formed with eight former students in 1983, wound up doing a fashion shoot for an Italian magazine. In a real sense, Coates's career is a product of media attention: it was pictures of his flat in a Japanese magazine that led to his first Japanese commission. Yet at a time when architecture in Britain is fighting a rearguard action against public, press and even princely hostility, and while most architects are keeping their heads low, Coates is prepared to explain what he stands for in terms that a wider public can understand. The magazines that profile him quite clearly find this sympathetic, and some of the most perceptive explanations of his aims and work have come from writers outside the architectural press.[3]

Despite his training and teaching at the Architectural Association, Coates is not a conventional member of the mainstream avant-garde represented by Peter Eisenman, John Hejduk and AA colleagues such as Bernard Tschumi (Coates's former tutor), Rem Koolhaas, Daniel Libeskind and Zaha Hadid. He doesn't take part in the international competitions which are their principal forum (though there are signs that this will change); and he is not, consciously at least, part of the much publicised

9

Above, Coates's Muse Britannia project of 1982 typifies his painterly approach. Fashion is another important source of inspiration. Right, Coates in the window of the London shop he designed for Jasper Conran

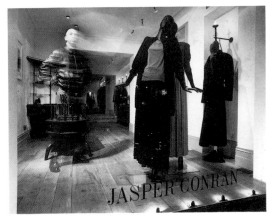

Deconstructivist tendency spotlighted by the exhibition at the Museum of Modern Art, New York in the summer of 1988 (though at least one writer, James Wines, has argued that his use of associative building archetypes and illogical fragments might qualify him for inclusion[4]). Stylistically, in any case, Coates's work could not be more different from the Deconstructivists'. His architecture evinces none of the geometrical purity and abstract architectonic obsession associated with Libeskind, Eisenman or Coop Himmelblau. In their cerebral constructions poised on the edge of spatial delirium there seems, at times, to be little room for the human subject. Coates's architecture, as Charles Jencks has noted, is a return to the language of expressionism.[5] It starts with the body and the nature of human events and swells outwards to enfold its users. Coates's lines have the curves of organic things rather than the perfection of the ruler; rough edges and flaws are allowed. He wants a sense of process and accretion that parallels the building in use. The only MoMA Deconstructivist whom Coates remotely resembles is Frank Gehry, with his somewhat comparable fragmentary assemblages, ad hoc treatment of materials and willingness to allow humour and sensuality into architecture. The other architects he admires, masters of

10

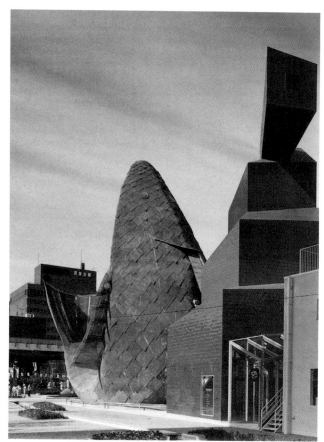

Like Frank Gehry with his Fishdance restaurant in Kobe, above, Coates has benefited from the Japanese taste for the outrageous. Left, the nursery he designed for an unpublished magazine feature on the Duchess of York

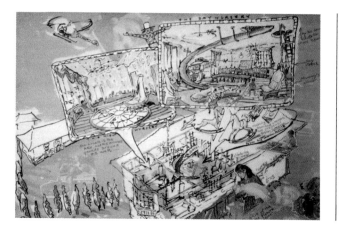

the temporary such as Shin Takamatsu and Toyo Ito, are Japanese, or Italian. The influence of Carlo Mollino and Paolo Deganello is particularly apparent in his designs for furniture.

More important to Coates, however, is the sense of belonging in London to a close-knit community of artists and craftspeople. Branson Coates's projects are always conceived as collaborations with teams of painters, sculptors, ceramicists, metalworkers, furniture and textile makers. Their objects aren't introduced as a layer of superfluous decoration once the serious architecture is finished; they form an integral, though inevitably slightly unpredictable, part of the "narrative" programme from the outset. Modernist notions of spatial purity and simplicity of finish are rejected in favour of layering, collage, reference and allusion, but the interiors are far from being haphazard; when paintings are removed or chairs are changed they suffer. What this curious late twentieth-century return to an Arts and Crafts aesthetic may presage, as a recent exhibition in Tokyo tried to argue, is a new phase in design where traditional crafts skills are combined with advanced manufacturing methods as a way of adding value (both financial and sensual) to functional objects.[6] At the very least, it

relates Coates's work to the broader currents of new British design in the 1980s; indeed his projects have provided an important outlet for some of its better-known representatives.[7]

Coates's readiness to draw in collaborators is typical of his and NATO's openness to the culture of the city beyond architecture – to street fashion, magazines, advertising, music, television, the visual arts and the new leisure technology. Not since the work of Peter and Alison Smithson with the Independent Group in the 1950s and of Archigram in the 1960s had a group of British architects been so willing to look to popular culture for techniques and inspiration. Like the Independent Group, NATO acknowledged no valid hierarchical distinction between high and low culture; for NATO, popular culture was intrinsic to lifestyle, and lifestyle, primarily in the form of their own subculture, was the issue their city projects attempted to address. Like Archigram, NATO used the popular medium of the magazine as a vehicle for their messages, developing graphic styles of considerable power (though markedly less coherence), which captured the mood of the mid-1980s just as richly as Archigram's op art collages and comic-strip futurism encapsulated the 1960s. Coates and NATO's exhibitions

11

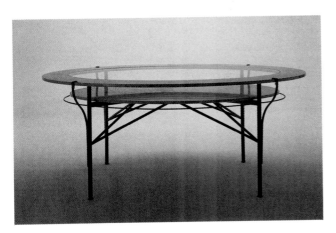

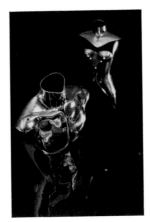

Left, Coates's Europa table, commissioned by Bigelli in Italy in 1989. Right, the male and female mannequins produced by Coates's own company, Omniate

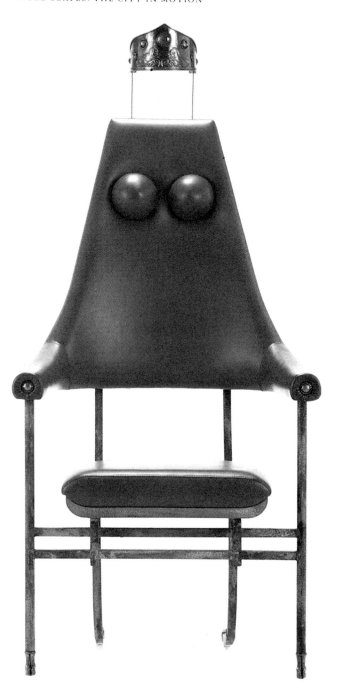

in London, Edinburgh and Boston were also never less than provocative. Indeed, NATO's appropriation of art forms – the painting, the object, the installation – was arguably too successful for their own good. Coates himself has developed a drawing style, using soft pencil or oil pastel and acrylics, of impressive fluency. Presented in the context of an art gallery, NATO productions were often indistinguishable from art, however much Coates and the group protested to the contrary. Consequently, art critics whose business was the imaginary had less trouble appreciating NATO's notional cityscapes as commentaries on urban living than some architecture critics to whom the group's primitive drawings and rubbish sculptures looked like fantasies that could never be built.[8]

Although themes of contemporary culture continue to inform Coates's work, his projects with Branson Coates show an interest in classical quotation that was never part of NATO's more streetwise agenda. At times, Coates's manipulation of this imagery strays perilously close to the "failed seriousness" Susan Sontag identified in her essay "Notes on 'Camp'" as typical of the form[9] – and for some commentators it more than crosses the line.[10] The Caffè Bongo, with its tarnished heroes on pedestals, seems

12

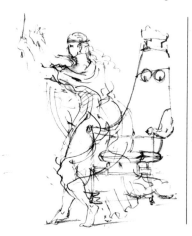

The Throne chair with built-in crown was one of a group of thirteen designs, many of them whimsical, put into production by the Japanese furniture company Rockstone in 1987. Left, an early sketchbook study shows the chair's classical origins

vulnerable to the accusation in a way that the Bohemia jazz club, devoid of classical flourishes, does not (one might note here that Coates himself prefers the latter). But even if the artifice, irrepressibility, extravagance, aestheticism and theatricalisation of experience of Caffè Bongo do make it camp, it is certainly far too knowing to be considered an example of pure or naive camp, which is by contrast, as Sontag noted, unintentional. Finally, perhaps, the "campness" of Bongo tells us as much about the society that commissioned and consumed it, as it does about Coates. And here Sontag, writing in 1964, might almost have been thinking of Tokyo in the 1980s: "Camp taste is by its nature possible only in affluent societies, in societies or circles capable of experiencing the psychopathology of affluence."[11]

The question boils down to the issue of style. If camp "incarnates a victory of 'style' over 'content'", is this what we discover in Coates's work? Coates and, for that matter, the rest of NATO have always denied that their method can be reduced to a single all-purpose "look". Instead, it is only by taking the styles of Coates's collaborators in combination – this Adam Lowe painting (five examples to date) and that André Dubreuil chandelier (three examples) – rather than by considering his own work,

that one might identify a Coates project. Remove the more revealing crafts contributions and nothing immediately links, say, the Jasper Conran shop, the Bohemia jazz club and L'Arca di Noè beyond a shared theatricality and, less obviously, a consistent approach to the treatment of the mechanics of space. On the evidence of his completed projects, one would have to say that content and, beyond that, method are more important to Coates than considerations of style. Coates's "narrative" approach to architectural imagery is above all a way of giving allegorical reinforcement to the function of a building. Working against the prevailing currents of international design – minimalist, post-modernist, Deconstructivist – yet still seeming acutely of his period, he has produced furniture, interiors and his first buildings in Japan. Does his work there have any lessons for design in the West? Is it even prophetic, as Coates suggests? Can a method suitable for a restaurant or a club be applied at the scale of the city? Before we can answer any of these questions, we need to trace the origins of narrative architecture back to Coates's work at the Architectural Association in the 1970s.

13

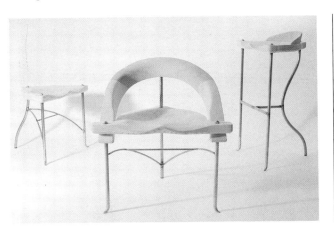

Coates's designs for the Arca di Noè restaurant in Sapporo, left, were introduced by the London company SCP in 1988. The underlying eroticism of Coates's furniture was never more frankly stated than in the Genie stool, right

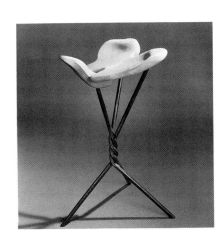

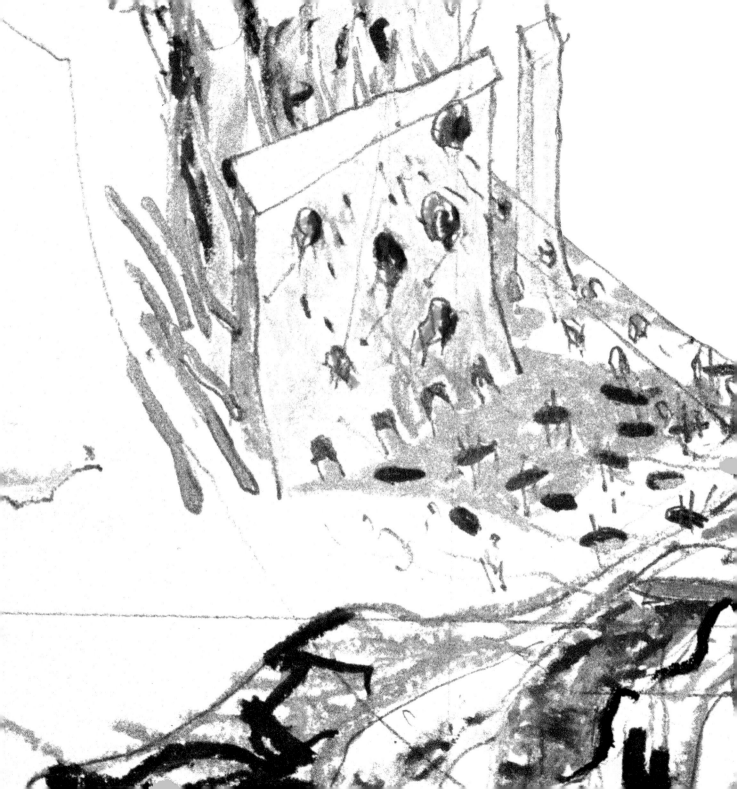

Chapter One | Diploma Unit 10

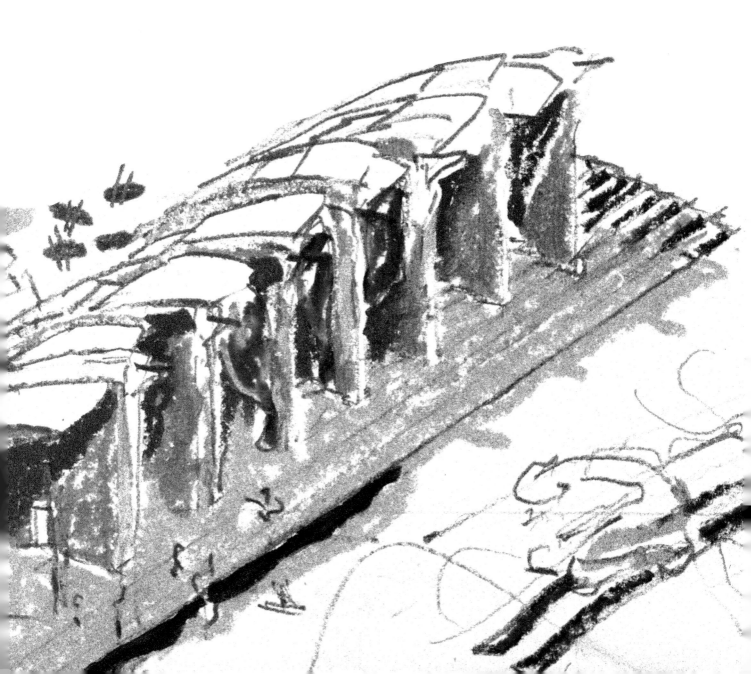

Nigel Coates was born on 2 March 1949 in Malvern, Worcestershire and was educated at Hanley Castle, a nearby grammar school. It was generally expected that he would go on to study engineering, but while taking a combination of science A-levels and art, Coates decided on architecture. After three years at Nottingham University, he moved to London to work in the architects' department of Lambeth Town Hall in 1971. He had no thought at that stage of continuing his studies at the Architectural Association, but gradually became aware of the possibility that he might attend. In 1972, having completed his year out, he entered the school.

The intellectual world he discovered could not have been more different from his studies at Nottingham. There, the emphasis was on formal and structural issues, sociology and sensitivity to the user. For his third-year degree project, Coates had designed an adaptable arts centre heavily influenced by the instant cities and plug-in fantasies of Archigram. But even at this early stage it was film language as exemplified in the work of Pier Paolo Pasolini that seemed to Coates to offer a more useful way of analysing architecture. In the hothouse atmosphere of the AA in the early 1970s, by comparison, the emphasis was not so much on the pragmatics of design as on the

pleasures of discourse. Students, like their tutors, were encouraged to take up, articulate and defend positions, and actual building, worrying about the beams and the lintels, was something that could happen later if at all. The AA was and remains internationalist in outlook, audience, students and staff. With the installation of the Canadian Alvin Boyarsky as chairman in 1971, a new mood of intensity and change swept through the economically rickety organisation. Boyarsky wanted its Bedford Square headquarters to become a forum, an arts workshop and a marketplace for ideas. Students could pick and choose between such contradictory propositions as the technological utopianism of Peter Cook and Ron Herron, the rationalism of Leon Krier, the surrealism of Mike Gold and the post-1968 politics of Bernard Tschumi.

Coates found himself drawn towards the latter. Tschumi, a French-Swiss who had been attracted to London by the vigour of late-1960s polemic, brought a philosophically inclined mind and an approach based in the visual arts to the processes of architecture. He introduced Coates and fellow student Jenny Lowe to the writings of the Situationists and to the related theories of the French sociologist Henri Lefebvre, whose *Everyday*

Previous page, detail of Coates's Ski Station project of 1981, one of a series of drawings in which he began to develop his distinctive high-energy style

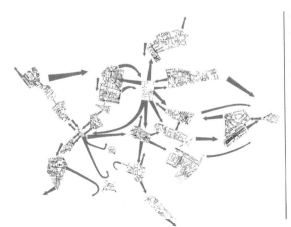

Guy Debord's Situationist map of "The Naked City". Situationist ideas about the "psychogeography" of the urban environment were a key early influence on Coates

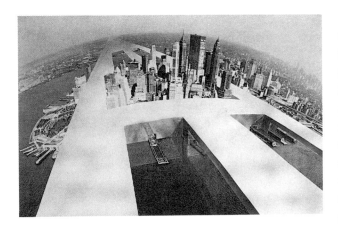

Life in the Modern World became a primer for Unit 2, the study group Tschumi formed in 1974.[1] From Lefebvre's post-Marxist critique they deduced the essentially simple idea that there was little point in designing architecture if it merely became an expression of the prevailing capitalist economy, thereby helping to perpetuate it. Nor did the answer lie in storming the citadel. Only when revolution had been effected on a cultural and personal level, in the transformation of everyday life, would architects have new criteria to apply. Or as Lefebvre put it: "Urbanism will emerge from the revolution, not the revolution from urbanism."[2]

But before Tschumi's vision of "subjective spaces and social playgrounds" could come about in the city, "space" itself would need to be redefined.[3] For Coates, notions of space borrowed from philosophers such as Hegel and Kant seemed, at this stage, to hold more expressive possibilities than did simply making symbolic representations of the city. "What was always more interesting to me was how to essentialise the nature of a spatial experience and then transfer it to the viewer. So it was always more an exercise in architectural communication than in making an observation about the nature of architecture as a thing separate from yourself."[4] Taking their cue from contemporary developments in conceptual and performance art, and from the example of radical Italian groups such as Superstudio and Archizoom, Coates and Lowe devised photopieces in which they photographed themselves in a variety of spatial and architectural settings. Their subjectivity and by implication that of the viewer was thus the core from which all other issues were addressed. In the Prison Park project, undertaken in his final year, Coates focused on the ironic circumstances of the typical park, where the landscape, standing in for the city itself, appears to signify limitless freedom, but where the individual's

17

Highly conceptual studies by the Italian group Superstudio, such as the Continuous Monument for Manhattan, above, suggested ways of using photographic imagery that Coates went on to apply in his Prison Park project of 1974, right

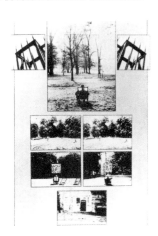
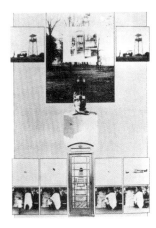
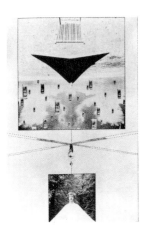

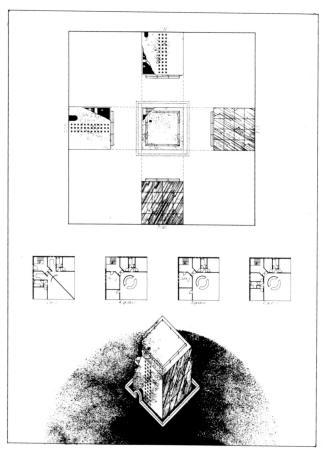

Coates and Branson's first collaboration was Royal Mint Housing, an entry for a Greater London Council competition in 1974. By nicking the gridded, cubic blocks at the corner, the pair questioned the conformity of mass housing

behaviour and capacity for movement are in fact controlled by a long list of regulations – appended by Coates to the photographic boards.

After graduating with a year prize in 1974, Coates returned to the AA to dabble in teaching for a year before Tschumi left for the US and the activities of Unit 2 came to a two-year halt. Supporting himself by occasional agency work, Coates continued to produce highly personal photographic projects, usually in collaboration with Antonio Lagarto, an artist friend. Lagarto's interest in formal gardens and Renaissance architecture proved to be a decisive influence. By the time Coates returned to the AA in 1977 to teach in Tschumi's renamed Unit 10, he was significantly closer to evolving a set of concerns and a means of expression that were truly his own. That year, he made his first attempt to apply some of his reading about Italian architecture when he entered a competition to design riverside housing for the Millbank Estate, next to Vauxhall Bridge on the River Thames.[5] Borrowing the plan of Palladio's Teatro Olimpico in Vicenza, itself a reconstruction of a Roman theatre, Coates visualised the flats as a sequence of theatre boxes overlooking the stage of the river. A pair of arches planted in the water "to suggest a certain axial

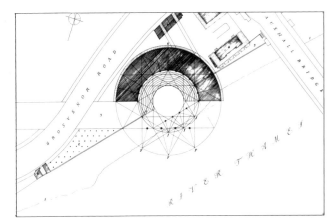

An Italian government scholarship to Rome University in 1978 gave Coates the opportunity to travel extensively in Italy, visiting historic gardens and theatres. The spatial issues that had preoccupied him in the most abstract way could now be reformulated, by reference to actual places, as a series of propositions about perspective, progression, circularity and enclosure. What intrigued Coates about the gardens in particular was the way in which space had been disposed and events staged so as to choreograph action, while leaving the walkers free to make their own choices. He explained: "Italian gardens work a bit like one of those arcade games that respond to which button you press: the narrative isn't prescribed. Whereas with a lot of English landscape gardens you start with one narrative idea and progress around the lake and there is only one way to go, the Italian ones had an exquisite, almost urban feeling of shuttling, like a pinball machine. The very simple grid structure formed on a slope would have extraordinary events at the ends of the avenues, with each condition handled in a very subtle way. But they would never lose sight of it being a simple path. They would have nuance, they would have attenuation, like a line of fountains on one side of a path which would brush the senses in a very particular way."[6]

discomfort" helped to direct the spectacle of the Thames towards its captive audience. To observers more accustomed to the conceptual intricacies of his photopieces, Coates's unabashed and seemingly retrograde manipulation of classical imagery came as a not entirely welcome surprise. For Coates, however, the imagery was intended, at this stage at least, to stand for nothing more controversial than "architecture"; more important was the way that the building concentrated and directed the relationship between audience – particularly the transient audience of riverside passers-by – and setting.

19

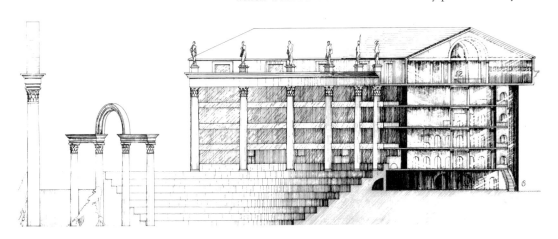

In the Millbank housing competition, Coates began to apply his reading about Renaissance theatres. The plan, above, reveals how the building turns against the axis of the river. Right, section showing classical columns and arches

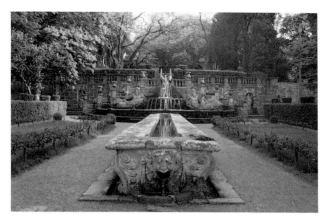

Programmatic considerations like these were given a more topical edge in the projects Unit 10 carried out in 1978–1980. In Soho Institutions, jointly formulated by Tschumi and Coates, the students inserted four incongruous building types – prison, asylum, stadium and ballroom – into a strip of nightlife London bounded by Neal Street and Wardour Street. Inspired by the writings of Michel Foucault, the asylum experiences of Antonin Artaud and the distorted sets of the expressionist film, *The Cabinet of Dr Caligari* (1919), the students produced architectural correlatives to confinement, madness, obsession and forbidden pleasure.

Many of their drawings were rendered in louring charcoals that seemed to be suffused with the malaise of punk London. As was his habit, Coates also undertook the project: "We wanted our designing to become forthright and expressive, for the distortions of the mind to be thrown out onto the buildings so that once built, they would throw some of the same feeling back. If architecture really were to have more than a guest/host relationship with the people that filled it, it would have to anticipate the way experience constructs its own narratives, constantly superimposing logic and emotion. Architecture, we said, should define an anthropomorphic field which constantly parallels and opposes experience itself. Like life, it had to aggregate and disintegrate the experiences it contained."[7]

In 1979, Coates took over from Tschumi as master of Unit 10. The Mayfair Squares projects he went on to set were the first to incorporate a live workshop (conducted by the Portuguese theatre director Ricardo Pais); it was designed to explore physical movement as a way of teasing out the possibilities of a particular space, in this case a studio. This less than conventional approach was taken a stage further the following year, in a workshop entitled "Modern Life in the City" which called on each

Gardens have provided Coates with complex models of spatial organisation. Above, a favourite example – the Villa Giulia in Rome, 1552. The watching figure of the herm, right, is also a key image. Far right, the garden as theatre: Cesare Ripa, 1758

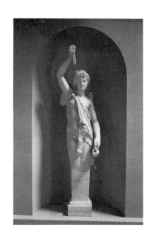

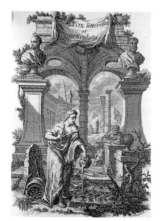

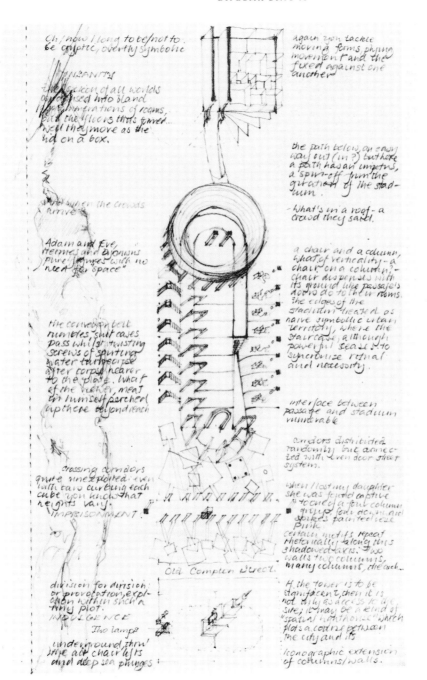

Coates's notebooks of the mid-1970s record his attempt to find a language appropriate to spatial experience. This sketch towards Soho Urbs (1978) is for his own version of Soho Institutions, a project he set the students of Unit 10

student to devise and act out a typical "modern situation". The bodily movements which resulted, best regarded as a sort of three-dimensional notation, were used as the basis of a design for a public space – car park, Underground station and so on. "The process involved standing in for the users of buildings and learning to use one's body as a source for an enriched handling of the elements of architecture and the real life situations which they contain," Coates explained.[8] Not that he meant to suggest that a literal translation of these gestures into architecture would be possible, still less that the spaces themselves might move or "perform". Nevertheless, he argued, "The very permanence of architecture can only be understood with the actions that take place in it as part of its structure. Then, and only then, can architecture entertain an intimate contact with the moment of perception – of being in it, of finding that it means something."[9]

During this period, Coates was becoming increasingly interested in the architectural implications of London's nightclubs. From mid-1970s punk clubs such as The Roxy in Covent Garden developed the "new romantic" clubs of the late 1970s and early 1980s – places such as Billy's, Blitz, Hell and The Beat Route. Coates was never

22

In a series of projects of the late 1970s and early 1980s, Coates explored the idea of the nightclub as a form of urban theatre. Nightlives of the Artists, right, proposed a subterranean disco for a Florence square

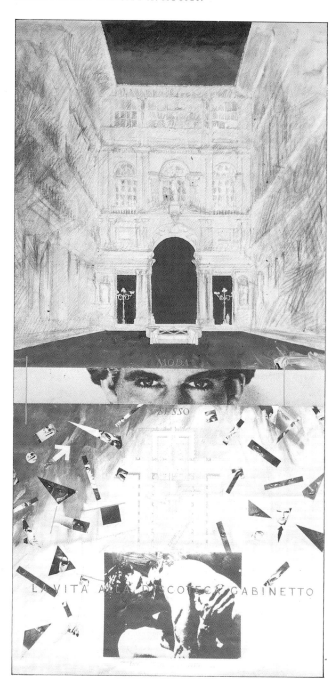

particularly involved in the musical aspects of this subculture, but the spectacle offered by these and more conventional clubs fascinated him. Nightclubs, he declared in an essay called "New Clubs at Large" in 1981, were the "protagonists of a current urban intensity".[10] The limitation of the architectural metaphor he had previously favoured, the theatre, was that it preserved the distinction between performer and audience; but clubs, by eliminating the spatial distinction between auditorium and stage, encouraging the "spectacle of the self" and promoting the "sensuous faculties of the body", turned everyone into a performer. This made them ideal environments in which to study what Coates described as the perceptual exchange between the body and the space it inhabits. In a personal project called Nightlives of the Artists, undertaken in 1979, Coates neatly montaged his classical and clubland interests by proposing a sort of disco mensroom, complete with pink strip lights, to be located under Vasari's Piazzale degli Uffizi in Florence. By contrast, the Fashion Airport project of 1980 (the title couldn't be more prophetic for his later work) was an attempt not to deny the city, as secret, subterranean clubs ordinarily do, but to affirm it. Nothing less than a completely new building type, according to Coates, this

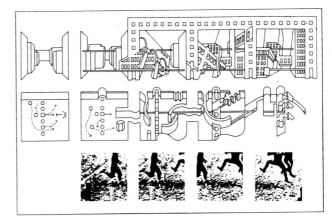

open-air nightclub was a delirious collision of street, catwalk, flying walls and triumphal arch in which the boundaries between body, clothing, gesture and building were intended to melt away.

Despite the ingenuity and restless experimentalism of such projects, the problem of how precisely to capture and transmit his perceptions in an architectural drawing remained. A number of Unit 10 students working on earlier projects had used forms of graphic notation derived from choreography and musical scores to plot the body's progression through architectural space. Tschumi would splice movie stills into sequences of drawings to

23

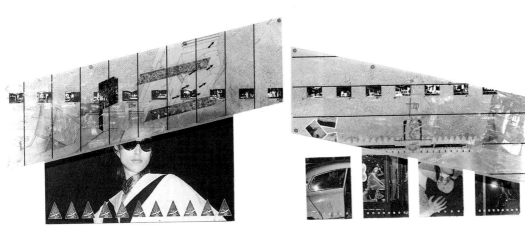

In the Fashion Airport project, Coates made use of film-like image sequences, similar to those favoured by Bernard Tschumi in projects of the same period, such as The Manhattan Transcripts, above

create architectural storyboards. The cerebral detachment of such methods didn't suit Coates, but neither, in the end, did his own progressively more sophisticated montages of photography and drawing. The answer came during a spell teaching at Bennington College, Vermont, in 1980. Immersing himself in the New York art scene, Coates became increasingly aware of the shift away from the cool, conceptual art practices of the previous decade (texts, cameraworks, performance pieces and video) towards a renewed interest in painting. It was an international tendency announced in London by the exhibition "A New Spirit in Painting" at the Royal Academy in 1981. For Coates, much of this art had an energy, a fury of expression, which he had edited out of his own work but desperately wanted to regain. He began to draw with new freedom, resisting his instinct to control the process and allowing the suggestions of architecture to emerge from his high-speed crayon scribble.

The first fruit of this new method was the Ski Station project, which he set himself and his Bennington students in 1981 after seeing a video with images of skiing by Nam June Paik. Coates had never actually been skiing, merely looked at the Bennington slopes when there was insufficient snow, but that didn't in any way inhibit the slithering momentum he brought to his drawings of the piste. The "pitstop architecture" of the ski run, the poles sunk into snow like rushing water and the hurtling, zig-zag descent of the skiers provided the perfect opportunity to elaborate the "ecstatic bond between body and raw landscape" and to overstate the "motifs of movement" in a way full of implications for his future projects.[11] After a decade of searching, Coates had discovered a way of representing architecture not simply as an object to be read but as an experience to be felt. He couldn't then have known how controversial it would prove to be.

24

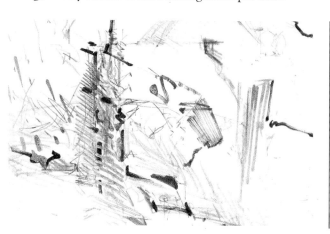

For Coates, the breakthrough to a new way of representing the sensations as well as the forms of architecture came with his drawings for the Ski Station. Left, original sketch. Opposite, two of the finished drawings

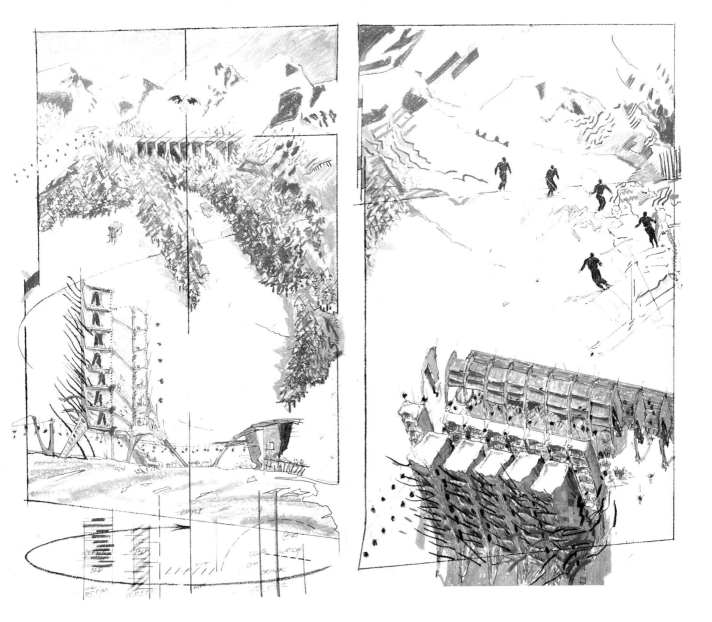

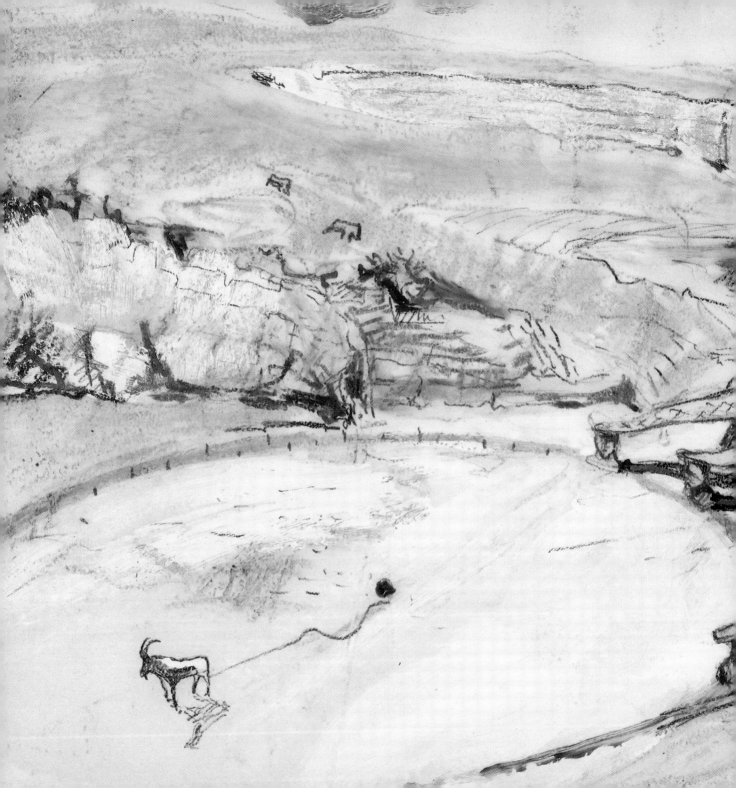

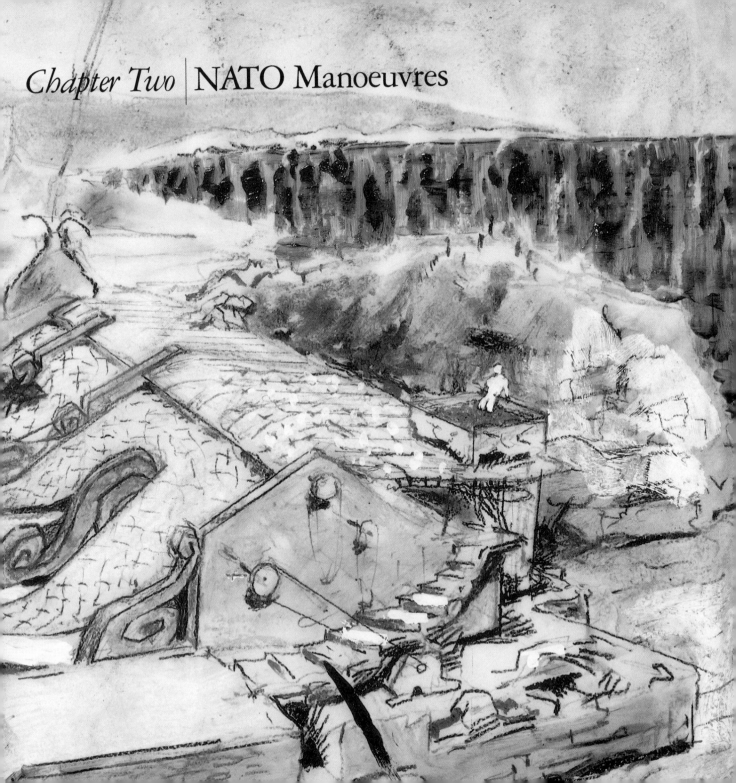

Chapter Two | NATO Manoeuvres

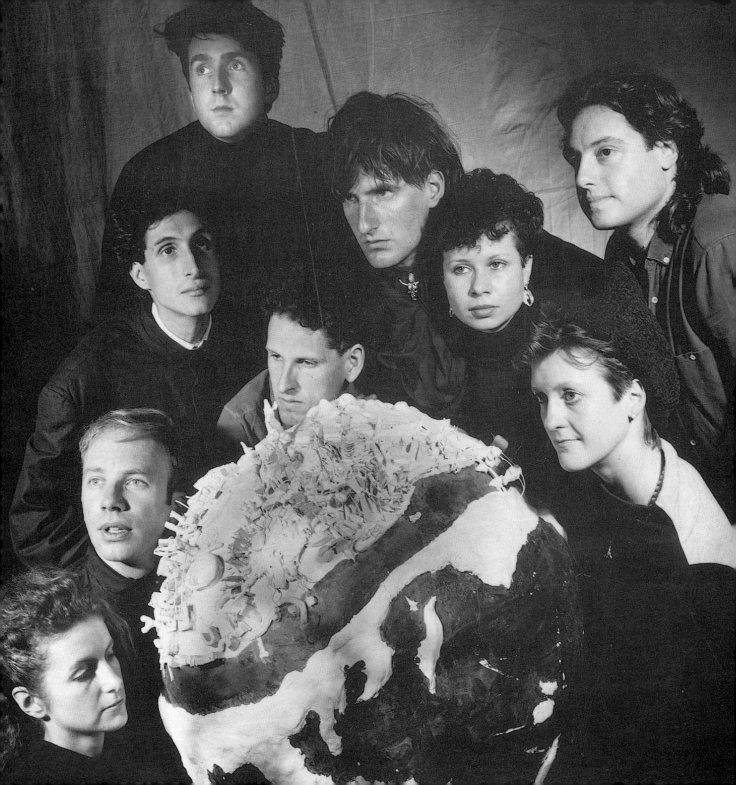

In the summer of 1983, the Architectural Association was in uproar. Something was going badly wrong in Unit 10 – or so it seemed. At the end-of-year assessment, visiting external examiners James Stirling and Ed Jones had looked through the work of nine of Nigel Coates's diploma students. On the basis of what they saw, they told the AA's diploma committee and assembled staff, they felt unable to pass any of them. The frenetic pastels and garish paintings made little sense to Stirling. "Each portfolio seems to be little more than a bunch of sketches with a few cartoons at the end," he is reported to have said.[1] To Stirling and Jones, the projects looked scrappy, unfinished, like an experiment still in progress. Where were the plans, the sections, the working drawings? Where, in short, was the architecture? Before any final assessment could be made a lot more work would evidently need to be done.

A second, emergency committee was hastily convened. AA chairman Alvin Boyarsky, Norwegian architect Sverre Fehn, Bernard Tschumi and Richard Rogers, chairman of the external examiners, took another look at the work. After lengthy deliberation and a reconsideration of earlier, more fully resolved projects, it was decided that Stirling and Jones's decision should be reversed: the nine students would, after all, be passed. Considering the unusual circumstances, they had all been incredibly lucky – some, perhaps, luckier than they deserved to be. But a more public form of vindication was clearly in order, especially after the incident made trade press headlines. Boyarsky suggested to Coates and the group that the work really did need to be taken a step further. It was time to answer the criticisms that had dogged the unit since Coates took over, by turning the sweeping social comment at which they excelled into buildable reality. A publication of some kind, financed by the AA, would be the obvious vehicle in which to do this.

Possibly Boyarsky envisaged nothing more provocative than a collection of working drawings. What he got was an unrepentant manifesto, as baffling to the outsider as the original projects and exhibition, and a fully fledged "organisation" into the bargain, consisting of Coates and eight former students – Catrina Beevor, Martin Benson, Peter Fleissig, Robert Mull, Christina Norton, Mark Prizeman, Melanie Sainsbury and Carlos Villanueva – three of whom (Fleissig, Benson and Villanueva) had not even been in the unit the previous year. The magazine they produced was called *NATO*, standing for "Narrative Architecture Today", and the group – unabashedly

29

Previous page, Coates's drawing of the house NATO designed for Derek Jarman. Left to right, Christina Norton, Nigel Coates, Carlos Villanueva, Robert Mull, Martin Benson, Mark Prizeman, Melanie Sainsbury, Catrina Beevor, Peter Fleissig

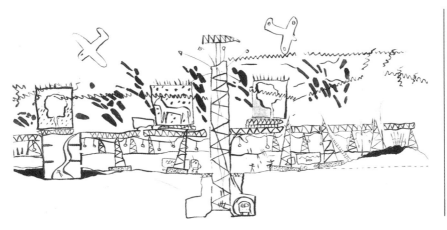

The examiners were baffled by the work Coates's students produced for their final-year project in 1983. Narrative images such as Robert Mull's drawing of Albion, left, bore little relation to conventional sections

situating itself "at the frontiers of architecture" – would thenceforward operate under the same name.[2] NATO's activities, as a statement inside announced, would range "from practice to product, from building to drawing, from vision to video, from talk to magazine". Its style was as brash, declamatory and at times downright impenetrable as its scope was ambitious.

In many ways, though, the choice of format could not have been more appropriate. The large tabloid pages of the magazine, the very fact that it was a magazine rather than some more formal, more purely architectural document and the way that it drew on the full repertoire of magazine techniques to engage (or enrage) the reader, made it a working example of the city phenomena NATO sought to transmit. The notable thing about the unit's work in the early 1980s had always been the degree to which it meshed with the circumstances of everyday life in the city – or the lives of the students and their milieu, at any rate. In contrast with the early days of the unit, this wasn't strained theoretical enquiry into the *vie quotidienne* so much as unbridled, hands-on participation. Coates and his students found quite as much to inspire them in art, pop music, fanzines, street fashion, nightclubs and the magazine culture of *The Face*

and *i-D* as they did in architecture – more perhaps. They were fascinated by the new gadgetry and software: computer games, video recorders, cashcard machines and Walkmen. And they knew all about the fragmentation of youth styles and the proliferation of lifestyle choices documented by Peter York in *Style Wars* (York himself came to talk to the unit in 1981[3]). Yet, at the same time, the group could hardly fail to be aware that these changes were taking place in a climate of biting recession, continuing industrial decline, accelerating unemployment and pervasive urban decay. The city itself was in trouble, and in Unit 10's view the stereotyped prescriptions of the planners, with their zoning restrictions and their bland determination to divide housing from leisure and the workplace from institutional life, could only add to the air of impoverishment and fatigue.

In a succession of projects dealing with particular areas of London, Unit 10 confronted these issues head on. For the Exhibition of Architecture brief that formed part of the unit's Modern Life project in 1981, Coates singled out Lansbury, the East End estate built in 1951 for the Festival of Britain. The following year, the group switched its attention to the Isle of Dogs, which became

30

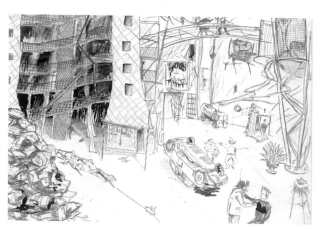

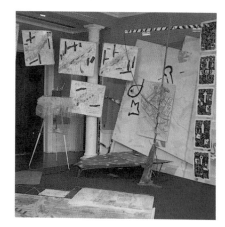

Mark Prizeman's Albion streetscene, left, caught the early 1980s' mood of inner city decay with obvious relish. The Albion installation at the AA, right, established a multi-layered approach that would become a hallmark of NATO's shows

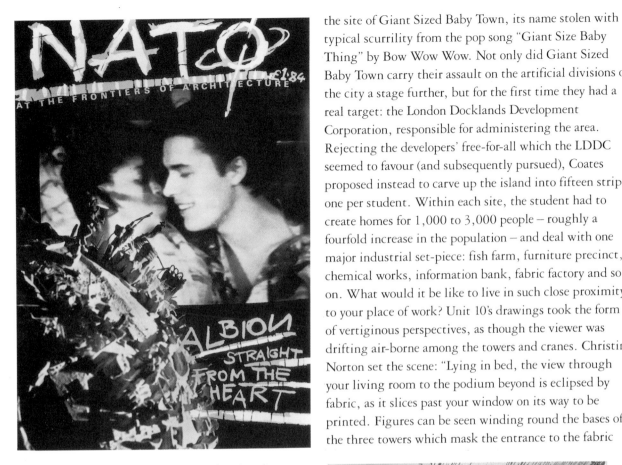

the site of Giant Sized Baby Town, its name stolen with typical scurrility from the pop song "Giant Size Baby Thing" by Bow Wow Wow. Not only did Giant Sized Baby Town carry their assault on the artificial divisions of the city a stage further, but for the first time they had a real target: the London Docklands Development Corporation, responsible for administering the area. Rejecting the developers' free-for-all which the LDDC seemed to favour (and subsequently pursued), Coates proposed instead to carve up the island into fifteen strips, one per student. Within each site, the student had to create homes for 1,000 to 3,000 people – roughly a fourfold increase in the population – and deal with one major industrial set-piece: fish farm, furniture precinct, chemical works, information bank, fabric factory and so on. What would it be like to live in such close proximity to your place of work? Unit 10's drawings took the form of vertiginous perspectives, as though the viewer was drifting air-borne among the towers and cranes. Christina Norton set the scene: "Lying in bed, the view through your living room to the podium beyond is eclipsed by fabric, as it slices past your window on its way to be printed. Figures can be seen winding round the bases of the three towers which mask the entrance to the fabric

31

NATO's first manifesto, above, was a knowing attempt to apply the methods of style magazines such as i-D, right, to the more staid world of architectural debate

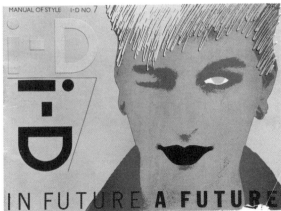

factory and the supermarket below. There, trucks are unloading raw materials and food. In the other direction, you can hear the clatter of the canteen mixed with the thudding pulse of the nightclub and the fervent shrieks of bargain hunters in the supermarket – all sounds measured against the background throb of machines."[4]

It was hardly surprising that observers not prone to attacks of industrial euphoria should have misgivings. The celebratory rhetoric recalled no one so much as Sant'Elia and the Futurists: "We are the men of the great hotels, the railway stations, the immense streets, colossal ports, covered markets, luminous arches, straight roads and beneficial demolitions."[5] Could Unit 10 be serious when it proposed that squares should become homes, homes factories, and that motorways should double up as playgrounds? The group's scrambled vision of conveyors cutting through kitchens and chemical pipelines shooting across living rooms was enough to scandalise the safety officers. But that quite probably was to miss the point. Giant Sized Baby Town had all the hallmarks of a giant-sized rhetorical exercise. Its expressionist distortions and dense urban layering, the wilful abandon with which it combined forms and mutated functions, were never intended to be read as a literal programme for

change. Instead, the town was a celebration of the possibilities of the city and an almost naively uninhibited argument for the rhythms, clashes and energy that make urban life attractive in the first place. Think of Venice, Manhattan or London's Soho, said Coates; compare them with the bland divisions of Le Corbusier's utopian *Ville Radieuse* or a British New Town such as Milton Keynes. "What planning as a principle ignores is the synthesising instinct of experience – that the proximity of dissimilar images and events can release architecture from its object status. This may be why most of us feel livelier in cities complicated by the imprint of one reality upon another."[6] By embracing industrial process and turning it into architectural spectacle for the "modern-minded artisans" who would work, shop and relax there, Giant Sized Baby Town might act as a catalyst for new ways of living.

Albion, the project that caused James Stirling such dismay, went even further. "Could the city truly be an active partner to the experiences it contained?" asked Coates in "Ghetto & Globe", the essay he wrote for the first issue of *NATO*.[7] Albion was an attempt to find out. Once again Coates had chosen a run-down and neglected area of riverside London, a wedge of land stretching from

Christina Norton's Education Line from Albion. The influence of Coates's own frenetic drawing style was obvious in the work of his students

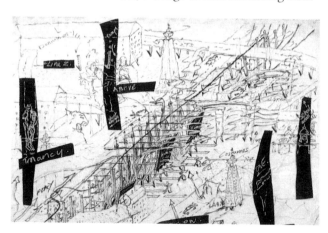

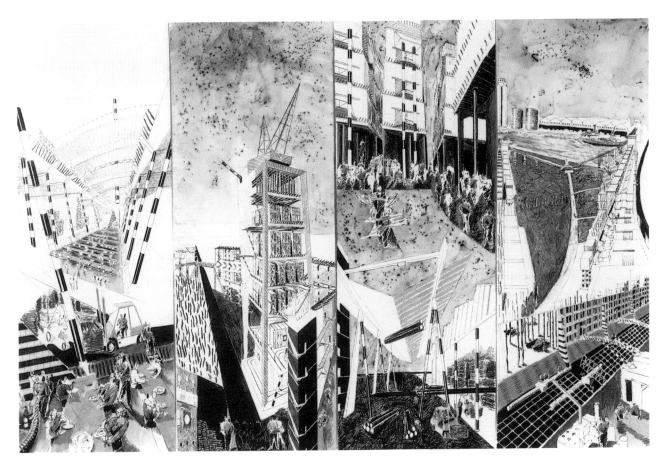

33

Carlos Villanueva's
Timber Fibre
Factory from
Coates's Giant
Sized Baby Town
project of 1982
had an industrial
vision heroic
enough to match
the noisiest
rhetoric of the
Futurists

London Bridge and Bermondsey to Rotherhithe and the Surrey Docks. Giant Sized Baby Town had taken a certain pleasure in the barren landscapes and ancient buildings of its site. Albion made it a point of principle to incorporate them, to weave the new city into the old without worrying if the joins were ragged or the stuffing showed. So much the better if the loose ends did show, because it was from the raw disjunctions, they believed, that energy and expression would flow. This was a philosophy of salvage and improvisation foretold by the Australian film *The Cars That Ate Paris* (1974), in which the delinquent townsfolk establish a micro-economy based on recycled car parts. So it was for some of the inhabitants of recessionary London. Why demolish what you could incorporate? Why discard what you could reclaim and re-use? Searching for comparisons with NATO's own methods, Coates pointed to Vivienne Westwood's piratical mixture of ethnic and traditional tailoring, and the customised ghetto-blaster, covered with horns, graffiti and aerials, which Malcolm McLaren used on the cover of the album *Duck Rock* in 1983.

But the parallels were wider even than this. In the 1950s, the British junk sculptors had dedicated themselves to what Eduardo Paolozzi called the "metamorphosis of rubbish". "CAR WRECKING YARDS AS HUNTING GROUNDS," declared Paolozzi, as he set about incorporating castings of broken clocks, dismembered locks and assorted wheels and electrical parts in his sculpture.[8] In the 1980s, the cultural landscape was full of people who might have been heeding his advice. In art and music, and on the fringes of design itself, the unwanted stuff of the city was being brought back to life. Sculptors such as Bill Woodrow and Tony Cragg combed the rubbish dumps for everyday materials they could use in their work. Andy the Furniture Maker found a steady supply of usable wood in abandoned buildings and yards, and Tom Dixon welded ancient pots and pans into light-fittings and chairs. Musicians such as Test Department beat out a doomy, industrial noise-music using hammers, drills, concrete and metal. Other gestures were grander still. The Bow Gamelan Ensemble, a performance group formed the same year as NATO, staged industrial *son et lumières* in the waterside wastelands of the city. Meanwhile, Joe Rush and the Mutoid Waste Company transformed the junkyard itself into a ramshackle machine for living in, surrounding themselves with the found-object totems of a new tribalism.

34

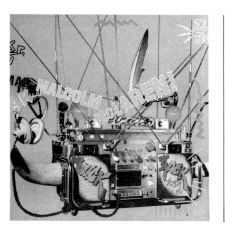

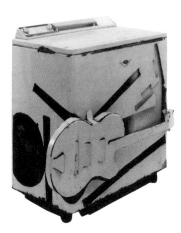

Malcolm McLaren's customised ghetto-blaster, left, encapsulated many of NATO's ideas about re-using the materials of urban life, as did Bill Woodrow's "Twin-tub with Guitar" (1981)

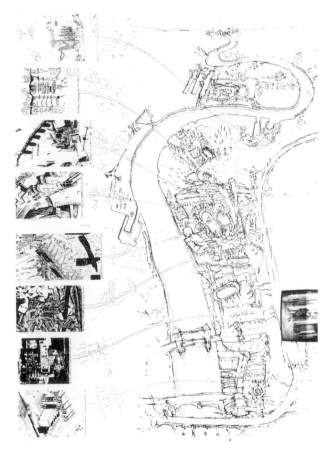

Above, spread from NATO 1, *showing Martin Benson's aerial view of Albion's riverside setting. The magazine's graphic style, right, had the rough-hewn, layered quality of the architecture*

Albion, too, began with objects cobbled together from city leftovers. One student, Mark Prizeman, built a chair featuring a cooking ring, a saucepan, an electric motor and a rubber mat; another, Christina Norton, made a mobile confession box on wheels with flashing lights. A video was then shot of each object and this in turn was used to generate ideas for the project. In the 1920s, the Surrealists would wander across Paris almost randomly in search of *le merveilleux*, and later, in the 1950s, the Situationists revived the art of purposeless drifting as a way of penetrating the mysteries of the city. The fledgling members of NATO used much the same technique to acquaint themselves with their individual plots of Albion. "Start from the way things work, what they feel like," urged a NATO slogan. "Instead of using plans, Albion builds on incidents, sometimes pulled from the underculture of the city as it stands, sometimes culled from the mind... The city grows outwards from the action that fires it, not inwards from the planners' city by numbers method."[9]

Thus would Albion cater to its citizens' needs; it was to be both ghetto (an enclosed, well-defined area) and globe (a universal city amplified, in the model NATO made, to cover the world). Its districts overlaid functions and

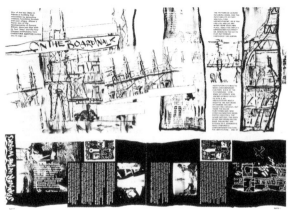

meshed together narratives in a provocative flux designed to cause meanings to slip and reverse. In this twisting, tatterdemalion city, architectural imagery could come from a neighbouring district – a dock crane or church tower – or from afar, as in the "zoo housing" devised by Mark Prizeman. In a bid to embrace the needs and oppositions found in cities everywhere, large-scale business resources incorporated their street-level mirror-images in a frank acknowledgement of the backyard economy. Albion's stock exchange and bank sat side by side with the betting shops; beneath the institutional computer tower there was a floppy disc library for home computer users; unemployment and the act of signing on at the labour exchange became opportunities for shopping; a tourist complex doubled up as film set. Far from trying to regulate its citizens or impose order on their lives through the patrician harmony of its planning, everything about Albion was designed to encourage misbehaviour and to liberate instinct – as the wild animal runs suggested. To live there each inhabitant would have to become a willing navigator in NATO's ever-shifting city of signs: "The new city must use every conceivable technique to flip meanings and throw the control of events back to the people performing them," as Coates put it.[10] And over it all, the architect – assuming levels of responsibility many would find alarming – presided as "moviemaker, social forecaster, artist and inhabitant".[11]

Despite the vigour of its polemical pronouncements, NATO was always more of a workshop than a talking shop. Its ideas arose from the group's practice of working together – making objects, assembling a magazine, putting together an exhibition – rather than from the dialectics of debate. The second issue of *NATO*, published in 1984, took as its theme this need to do it yourself, to become a modern "apprentice" or artisan as a city survival tactic. It attempted to show that anyone could apply NATO's architectural ideas to the production of everyday objects – that with a little imagination, some bent metal and a sheet or two of corrugated iron you too could "Albionize your Living Room". Where the first issue had been edited by Coates in his role as former tutor, the second was edited by the entire group. In its diversity, *NATO 2* was more like a conventional magazine, and that perhaps was its weakness. It had an interview with "mutant preacher" Joe Rush, a statement by "new world constructor" Jasper Morrison and an article on Britain's industrial landscape by NATO's critic in

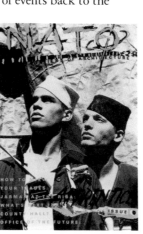

In the second issue of the magazine, Coates and the group's fashion interests moved to the fore. The theme was artisanal

residence, Brian Hatton. A photo-feature highlighted the group's growing interest in the world of fashion (not all of the members approved). In place of a single, central project the issue offered a round-up of members' recent work, including "ArkAlbion", Coates's solo exhibition at the AA,[12] and NATO's (unbuilt) designs for a house for the film-maker Derek Jarman — the only time that each of the members contributed to the whole design, rather than designing one of the parts.

By 1985, NATO's volatile cocktail of art, fashion and architecture was attracting as much attention outside the architectural community as it was inside it. After all, the group had all the characteristics of an avant-garde art movement in miniature. The manifestos, slogans and shock tactics, the strong sense of group identity and, in time, even the obligatory expulsions were deeply gratifying to an audience familiar with the life cycles of modern art's great isms. Initially the degree of interest NATO generated took some of the members by surprise, but under the direction of Coates, a media natural, they quickly learned how to play the publicity game. Born in media controversy, NATO became a media event. In November–December 1985, the group was invited to exhibit at the Air Gallery, London, by Iwona Blazwick,

an art world sympathiser. "Gamma-City", the installation that resulted, was the most complex, demanding (and, for the Arts Council, expensive) of NATO's manoeuvres to date, yet it saw the group making greater efforts to summarise its narrative method. "NATO's Gamma-City is a get-up-and-go starter pack based on typical sites and probable events. It scrambles uses and meanings... it bends stereotypes... it uses double levels... fictions are used politically. Its city is made active again, putting back the movement that Modern Movement Man forgot about. Why Gamma? Because gamma-rays emit spontaneously. They radiate strong short radio waves, effecting built mutations."[13]

In the accompanying issue of *NATO* magazine, which functioned as a catalogue, Coates recommended six surefire ways to effect these mutations: "Think of an intermediary architecture on that edge between people's lives and the given city, a kind of city furniture poised to refurbish rather than rebuild.... The interweaving of diverse functions should be seen as positive. Hence look upon tangled road-rail junctions, building sites and converted factories as Gamma-places built by accident.... Unpick the situation until bare signs show through, then expand them and spread them out to make space really work as a trigger for experience…. Build in fictional gestures and narrative sidesteps, because peripheral ingredients can upgrade reality when thrown in with it…. Customise situations with new means and new technologies, not as futurology, but as taking stock. Tape decks, discdrives and VTR's have outgrown their status as commodities. They're spare parts of the architecture of our daily lives…. Use materials to exploit their differences. Bend them, stretch them, paint them and erode them, use their contortions to build impulse into dynamic form. We want sensual architecture, architecture which stimulates."[14]

In 1911, the Futurist Umberto Boccioni had painted "The Street Enters the House", a fusion of spaces more perceptual than actual. NATO set about disrupting the divison between the detached, cultural preserve of the Air Gallery and the architecture of the street with an even more iconoclastic disregard for boundaries. In order to bring the exhibition into the street, they draped the facade with scaffolding and rubbish chutes as though the gallery was in the process of refurbishment (the effect can be seen in the film *Mona Lisa* in which the gallery is briefly visible). To make the street enter the gallery, the zebra crossing which runs up to its door was

extended across the floor inside. "Gamma-City" was divided into "marketplace" and "boudoir" to provoke further reflections on the interpenetrating realms of public and private space. There were perspective drawings and sections on the walls, some of them familiar from previous NATO projects, but none of the plans, maps or scale models one might expect to find at an exhibition dealing with urban issues. Instead, NATO's workshop methodology ran riot in a tangled and menacing profusion of objects lashed together from city cast-offs, each one an attempt to encode the "narratives" drawn from a particular London site: Battersea goods yard, Brixton market, the Thames Barrier, Cannon Street station, Southwark cathedral, the Old Street roundabout and so on. But first came NATO's Albion globe, orbiting above the Gamma-City, a collage model of matted debris trailing from an antelope's skull, which cascaded down from the ceiling on a wave of plastering mesh. Moving on past the Fish Flap columns fashioned by Robert Mull from posts covered in clay and hung with corrugated iron doors, the visitor arrived at a BSA motorbike and sidecar filled with onions by Mark Prizeman. Opposite was Prizeman's makeshift, fictional Gunfetish Club and next to that, by a heat-rippled perspex Weirwall, Carlos

38

At the Air Gallery, London, NATO demonstrated their narrative method to a wider public, using a barrage of three-dimensional devices. Right, the Gamma globe swings over a model of the city. Far right, a zebra crossing enters the "marketplace"

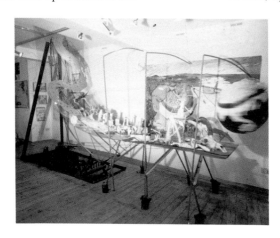
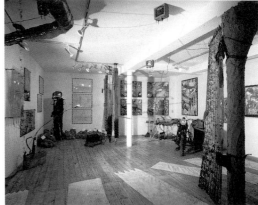

Villanueva had rigged up a burnt railway sleeper to act as a plinth for a ravaged VDU. Overhead, toy televisions announced NATO slogans: "Gamma-City is not a style but a political, social and aesthetic attitude based on scrambling signs and processes.... Exchange is a basic act of architecture, and its space the street. Gamma streets double up as home, market, factory, bar, switching old images for new uses.... See possessions, objects, furniture, clothes, as urban toys."[15] Upstairs, in the "boudoir", were further Gamma mutations. Catrina Beevor's surgical tubing chandelier floated like a jellyfish above Melanie Sainsbury's laboratory equipment place-settings on Mark Prizeman's boardroom table fitted with bandaged-tripod legs. Peter Fleissig had constructed Savage Furniture from slabs of plywood, sheets of galvanized steel and industrial clamps, while Coates's Wombat wardrobe, a soft accessory, clung to the wall nearby. The physical presence of these assemblages was so compelling that the architectural images on the walls, as frenzied and expressive as ever, seemed almost beside the point.

Reactions to "Gamma-City", which transferred to the Fruitmarket Gallery, Edinburgh in April–May 1986, were predictably mixed. Iwona Blazwick, as organiser, was delighted with the exhibition's provocations. Invoking the Surrealists rather than more scientifically minded city planners, she had predicted in *NATO* 3 "a vehicle for dreams and chance encounters".[16] "What was really exciting about it was that it had an incredibly startling visual effect. Instead of being very pristine and clean it was dirty, it was ragged, it was aggressive and it encompassed everything. It went from graphics to fashion and it was very much about the street. It seemed to go in the way that architecture should go – it touched upon its environment and its cultural context."[17] Examining the question of cultural context, Brian Hatton voiced a similar but slightly more guarded enthusiasm for the Gamma method. For Britain, he argued, the days of the "grand design" are over; what the British are good at now is scripting particular bits of the total picture – just as NATO had devised a new script for filling in the gaps in the existing city: "British cities have always tended towards the condition of an empirical heap. Why not turn these habits into virtues: urbanize the pastoral, resite the idyll, industrialize the picturesque, and put the city back into 'garden city'?"[18] Perhaps, suggested Hatton hopefully, the techniques developed by subcultural groups could be extended to our national

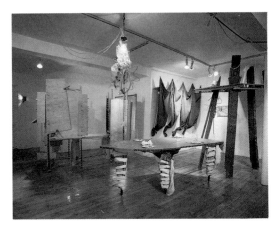

The upstairs "boudoir" section of "Gamma-City", with Savage Furniture by Peter Fleissig, table by Mark Prizeman, chandelier by Catrina Beevor and Wombat wardrobe by Coates

39

institutions. Even then, the viability of such a vision would very much depend on the extent to which a future society found a need for "the uses of enchantment" proffered by NATO.

But one critic's empirical heap is another critic's rubbish dump and for some there was nothing enchanting about NATO's anarchic anti-planning. By romanticising decay, said the sceptics, the group wasn't so much facing up to gritty reality as ducking the opportunity to make cities better; and only slum clearance and the will to start again could accomplish that. In 1983, Jules Lubbock had taken Albion to task for ignoring the views of its local population.[19] With "Gamma-City" the critic Peter Dormer took a tougher line. "Accepting obsolescence by making a live-in collage of the slums that are our cities looks OK only on paper. Living in a slum is in a sense 'more real' than living in genteel refurbishment, but it is like refusing to treat an abscess on the tooth on the grounds that the pain is a reminder that you are still alive."[20] Opening up the institutions of finance, the law and education to public access was an attractive idea, but it could never happen. In reality, said Dormer, "The NATO city would be like Beirut in a ceasefire."

40

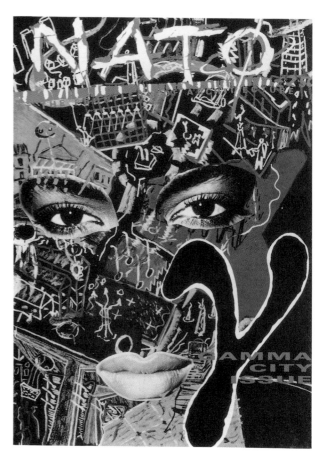

The third, Gamma-City issue of NATO, above, was the most graphically inventive, mixing drawings, fashion photography and printed slogans to suggest how buildings and streets too might "overlap", left

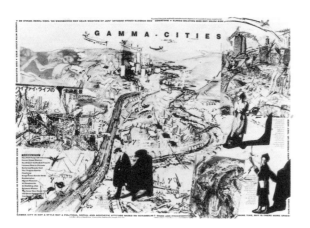

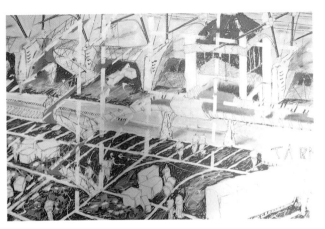

41

In Coates's East
meets West vision
of Gamma Venice,
the Peggy
Guggenheim
museum becomes a
trade centre. Left,
Tarmac 2 by Carlos
Villanueva, also
from the
"Gamma-City"
show

If NATO's later visions were intended simply as literal blueprints for the new city, it would be hard to fault this judgement. With hindsight, however, most of NATO's personnel deny their projects were ever meant to be read in this way. For Coates, the junkyard expressionism that might to some people suggest alienation, disgust or despair (and in modern art it often has) represented nothing more disturbing than "passion" and an untrammelled effusion of energy. "The true modernism", Susan Sontag has written, "is not austerity but a garbage-strewn plenitude."[21] NATO, to judge by its practice, would seem to agree. The industrial entrails, the cannibalised technology, the scrapmetal entropy, even the deathly antelope skull, were merely devices in an armoury of narrative effects, along with the distortions, overstatements, extrapolations, transformations and implausible conjunctions of the drawings.

In an important sense, though, whatever NATO claim and whatever their talents as polemicists, the real architectural implications of their proposals were never finally resolved. The group was always a prey to minor disputes, jealousies and tensions. After "Gamma-City", three of its members – Melanie Sainsbury, Christina Norton and Martin Benson – were asked to leave. From the outset, all nine had been involved in projects of their own and Coates, in particular, was increasingly preoccupied by commissions. "Gamma-City" was consequently the final issue of the magazine and NATO did not regroup for another exhibition until 1987. Even then, although Coates was involved in the planning of NATO's Heathrow airport installation for "The British Edge" at Boston's Institute of Contemporary Art, he was unable to travel to the US to help build it. NATO's exploration of "terminal culture" was ingenious and spectacular, making use of drawings, paintings, sculptures, videos, found objects and airport equipment, but very much a recapitulation of earlier themes, as one of its slogans suggests: "Think of this gallery as an architectural space between countries. An airport is like a citadel nestling amid suburbs of its own domain – a ghetto on the globe with a transient population of 40 million travellers a year. It acts as a model of the world, revolving around passport control."[22] For NATO, Heathrow was already layered like one of their own narrative projects, adapted and built over to the point where it had become an example of twentieth-century archaeology that enshrined the "contemporary mythology of air travel".[23] Now, they argued, it must face up to its

42

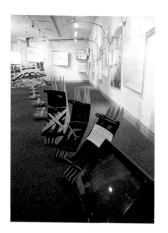

NATO's Heathrow installation at the Boston Institute of Contemporary Art was an elaborate attempt to evoke and analyse the modern airport, using everything from "sombrero" landing lights, left, to video screens, right

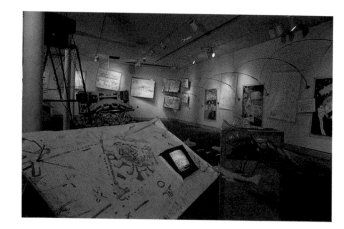

role as gateway, fortress, dormitory, trading exchange and "cosmopolitan crossroads". The exhibition was widely reviewed in the US and warmly received, but it proved to be the last such collaboration by the group.

So should NATO in the end be regarded as anything more than a particularly vivid style, bound to a moment in British cultural history which has now passed? Recognising that this might happen, NATO were always insistent that what counted was their method: "Gamma-City is not a style but a political, social and aesthetic attitude based on scrambling signs and processes." But many onlookers, impressed by the physical signature of their work, the brutal structures and rapid-fire drawings, have failed to grasp the method and savoured, or copied, only the style. It is even possible that the style, and the way it caught the *Zeitgeist,* was the most telling aspect of NATO's output. By denying us further productions under the group name but in different styles, more appropriate for the present, the group has made it difficult to be sure. Some members argue that they are applying the lessons of narrative architecture, albeit at a fairly simple level, in commissions for domestic interiors and restaurants. Three of them teach at the Architectural Association. Mark

Prizeman, possibly the most undeviatingly NATO-esque of all the members, tutors first-years and, in 1988, Robert Mull and Carlos Villanueva (now Villanueva Brandt) took over from Coates as leaders of Diploma Unit 10. Under their leadership, emphasis has shifted away from the art strategies favoured by Tschumi and Coates towards a more hard-nosed consideration of finance, development and economics, topics largely neglected by NATO. But it is in the output of Coates himself, working with his practice, Branson Coates Architecture, that the narrative techniques jointly developed with his former students have achieved their most sustained and concrete expression to date.

43

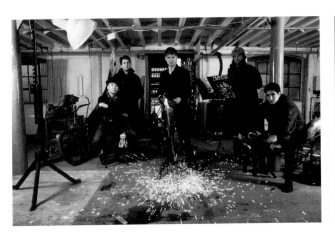

A workshop ethic was always central to NATO's projects. Pictured from left to right, Coates, Mull, Prizeman, Fleissig and Villanueva in 1987, when the group was down to six (Catrina Beevor is missing)

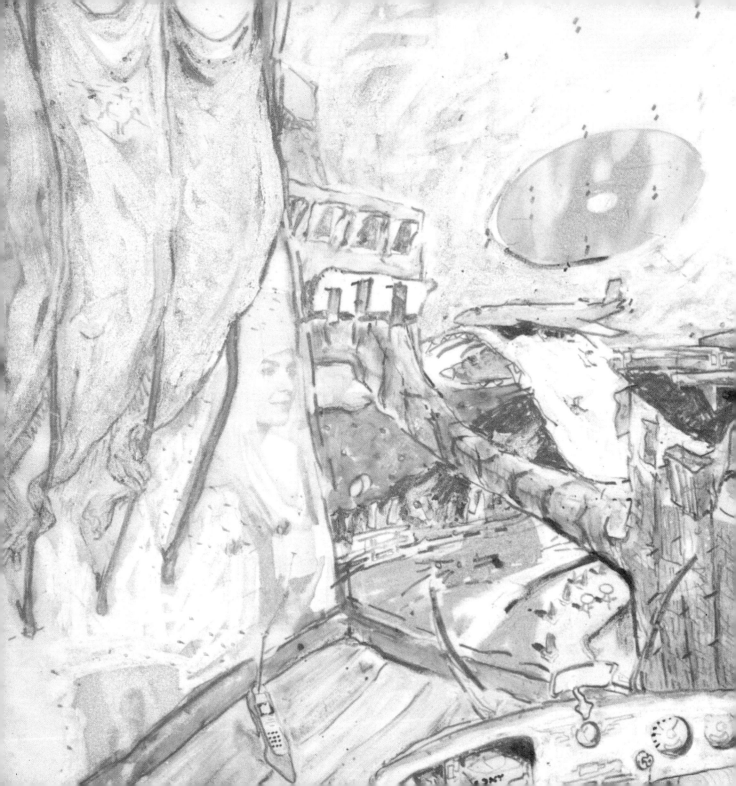

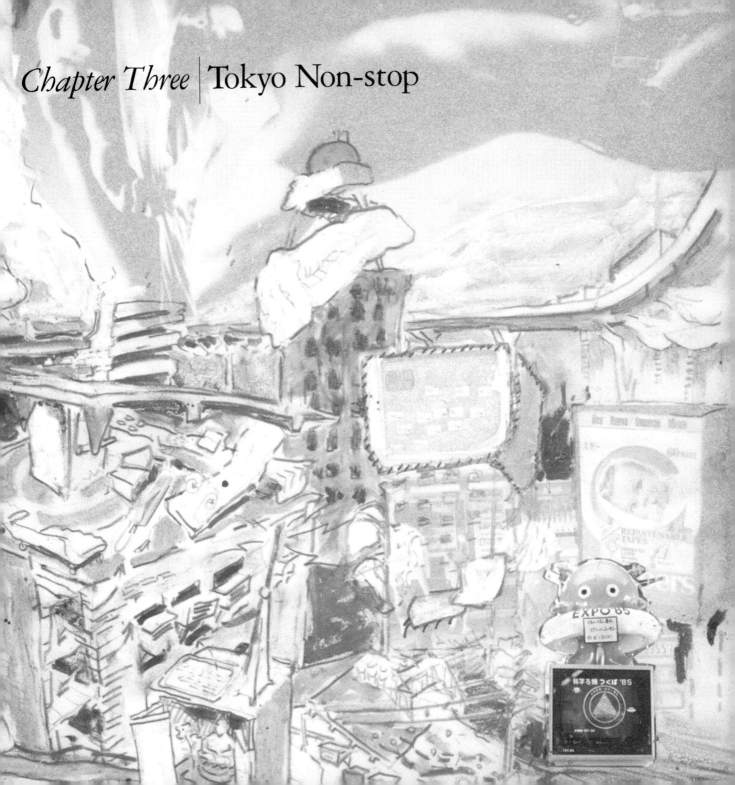

Chapter Three | Tokyo Non-stop

If Nigel Coates's Japanese projects have the quality of a dream, so does the means by which he came to design them. One day in 1984, a Chinese entrepreneur based in Tokyo came to the door of his home. He said he had seen pictures of Coates's flat in a Japanese magazine, *Brutus*, that he liked them very much and that now he wanted to work with Coates on something similar in Japan. He talked impressively of office projects, restaurants and shops, and mentioned a castle conversion. Coates, naturally enough, expected nothing to come of this. It sounded impossibly distant and implausible and, in any case, for the past ten years he had lived the life of a "paper" architect, thinking, teaching, drawing and writing about architecture. Apart from his own flat – a collaboration with Antonio Lagarto – and a domestic interior for the fashion designer Jasper Conran, which he was working on at the time, he had built nothing. The only signs that he had ever contemplated designing a real rather than notional building were his designs for a Greater London Council housing competition in 1974, and entries for the Millbank housing competition in 1977 and the Paris Opera House competition (with Martin Benson, Carlos Villanueva and Peter Fleissig) in 1983.

Six months after the visit, Coates was in Tokyo working on an idea for a restaurant with his new Japanese contact, Shi Yu Chen. Originally Chen planned to finance the project himself (he had owned a gallery-restaurant in Los Angeles), but when the money ran dry another backer was found. Chen called his new company CIA, short for Creative Intelligence Associates, in obvious emulation of the global reach suggested by NATO's acronym. As one of the first of a new breed of self-styled "creative producers", Chen aimed to match designer and Japanese client in a way that neither would have managed independently. His role took in the more conventional responsibilities of project management, but it began with the development of the design idea and extended through all phases of the creative life cycle. For Tokyo companies suffering from data paralysis in the most information-intensive city in the world, Chen acted as a kind of filter. It was his job to anticipate what the client needed, to discover the talent to realise these visions, and to translate Western and Japanese cultures into terms the other could understand.

Coates was obliged to start a new company to handle the demands of his first major commission. In April 1985, he teamed up with Doug Branson, a colleague from his student days at the AA (they had collaborated on

46

Previous page, detail of Gamma Tokyo by Coates captures the restlessness and energy of one of the world's most image-saturated cities

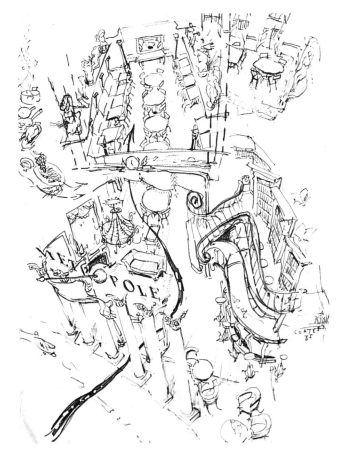

the GLC housing competition), to form Branson Coates Architecture. Coates is the primary designer and Branson is more efficient at handling administration, contracts and technical tasks, but roles remain fluid. Coates's designs incorporate ideas from Branson, while Coates, far from being an impractical fantasist, has a talent for detailing. Later, they were joined by Anne Brooks, who became the third member of the management team, also responsible for co-ordinating the activities of Omniate, a second company formed to handle purchasing. Branson Coates's first office was a former shop in a quiet Pimlico street, a fax machine their twenty-four-hour lifeline to Tokyo. When they ran out of space in 1987, they moved to light industrial premises in Clerkenwell.

Chen's original idea for the Metropole, as it came to be called, was that it should mix together elements of an English gentleman's club and a European café with traces of the "decay" he had admired in Coates's flat. It was to be an exercise in rampant nostalgia, serving Chinese food with knives and forks to the Euro-conscious clientele who flocked through the streets of Roppongi, a highly fashionable nightlife district with the greatest concentration of foreign visitors in Tokyo. This rather literal conception of authenticity was hardly sufficient to 47

Above, Coates's drawing of the Metropole, Branson Coates's first Japanese project, showing bar, balcony library, restaurant and private dining room, back right. Right, sketchbook detail of the facade

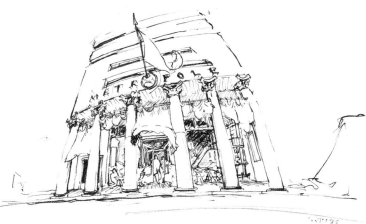

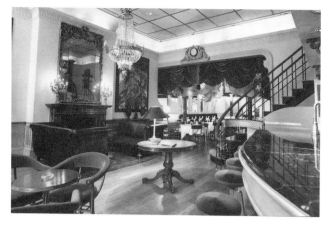

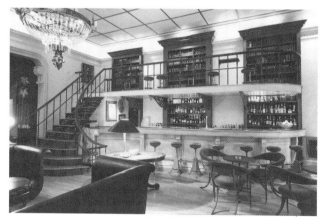

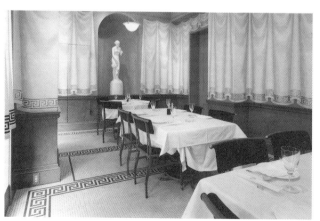

satisfy Coates, so he added a number of overlapping "narratives" of his own: artist's studio, theatre, library and orangery. A substantial purchasing budget meant he was able to bring over British antiques to flesh out the fiction. There was an embassy flagpole, doors salvaged from demolition sites, a marble fireplace from a City of London post office, plaster casts of Mercury, Achilles and other mythological figures, and stacks of second-hand books for the library above the bar. Hoping to project a sense of London's creative community through the scheme, Coates commissioned artists and craftspeople to provide objects and pictures. Tom Dixon constructed the first of several chandeliers for Coates, as well as bent metal capitals for the colonnade; Adam Lowe made allegorical paintings for the bar (subsequently removed by the client); Edward Allington did a drawing; Zaza Wentworth Stanley painted the pelmets; Valerie Robertson executed brass castings for the furniture; and Michael Scott and João Penalva used special paint finishes to give the walls of the converted garage that the restaurant occupies a patina of old age.

The result was a fantastical stage set whose tongue-in-cheek grandeur and camp theatricality were only heightened by the proscenium and billowing swags

The Metropole has the faded elegance of a gentleman's club, with English antiques, furniture by Coates and the work of London artists. A painted proscenium turns the dining room, opposite, into a theatre for eating

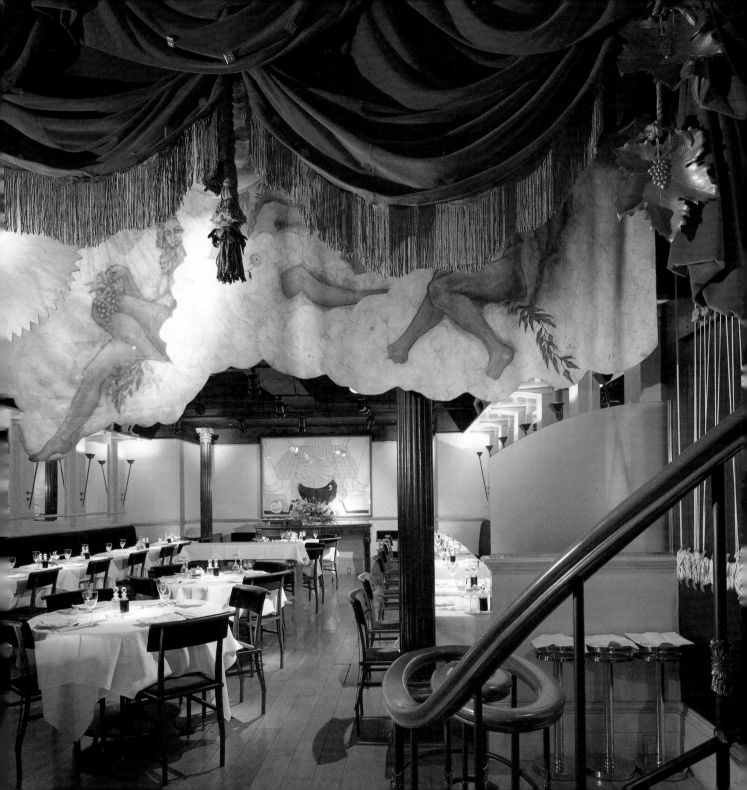

Coates used to divide the bar from the dining area at the back. It was an oriental dream of a time and a place that have never quite existed, realised with an attention to detail that only the Japanese could muster. From the British point of view, as Dick Hebdige has noted, this outpost of some forgotten empire had about it the air of a "seance" convened with a collection of "ghostly presences", which carry with them "the traces of their earlier contexts and uses, their other former lives".[1] The Metropole opened in December 1985, not long after "Gamma-City", and its meticulously confected elegance was hard to reconcile with NATO's mutated city visions. Coates spoke eloquently of how a certain Japanese taste "aspires to the atmosphere of European buildings in a state of resonant decay", but for some of the other NATO members it represented a step back to an earlier way of working.[2] It had, after all, come out of the distressed classicism of Coates's own flat rather than the last three years of work. And in NATO terms it didn't seem to go far enough. Other members, such as Carlos Villanueva, who worked on the project with Coates, might have bolted the beautiful cornices two inches off the wall, or put them on the floor rather than the ceiling – played with the signs in some way by inverting expectations.

But for Coates, in the Metropole a cornice was a cornice: it went, with all due decorum, exactly where you would expect it. Even Coates seemed sensitive to the contradictions. "The Metropole's visual vocabulary is built on archaeological references and functional allusions, but its method of dynamic assembly is quite separate," he wrote in the summer of 1986. "It could work just as well with aircraft shapes and industrial objects as it does with classical staging. We'll prove this with our next crop of jobs in Japan."[3]

By then the Metropole was drawing trendy Tokyoites in off the street and work was well under way on two further projects in the city. Coates was flying regularly to Tokyo and the element of autobiography in the crashed aircraft wing interiors of Caffè Bongo and the Takeo Kikuchi building was unmistakable. In interviews (and there were many interviews after the Metropole opened), he liked to talk of the city as a "cultural airport lounge", a nice image for the visitor's sense of jet-lagged amazement at the immensity of this international melting pot for trends and fashions. The Japanese were receptive, it seemed, to the most outlandish architectural ideas – ideas that, back in London, were impossible to realise. Indeed, they embraced them as an economic

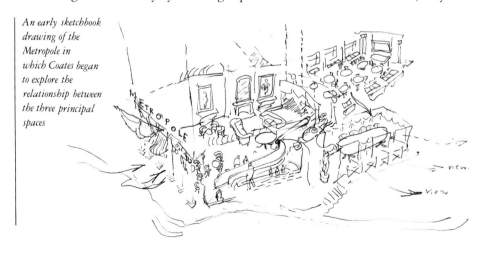

An early sketchbook drawing of the Metropole in which Coates began to explore the relationship between the three principal spaces

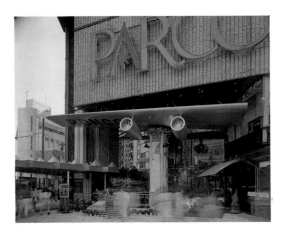

Coates's drawing, above, visualised the Caffè Bongo as a cauldron of centripetal energy. The original entrance is under the lower wing flap on the right. Bongo needed external drama to compete against the city around it, right

Overleaf, Caffè Bongo's interior was like nothing that had been seen in Tokyo before. It was as though an aircraft wing had crashed and merged with classical ruins, with Fellini in charge of the mise-en-scène

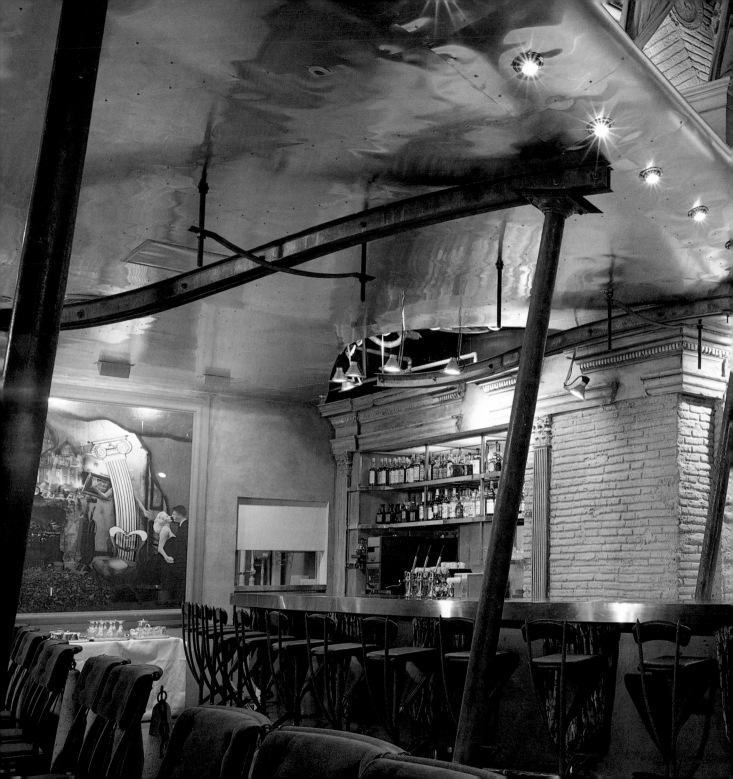

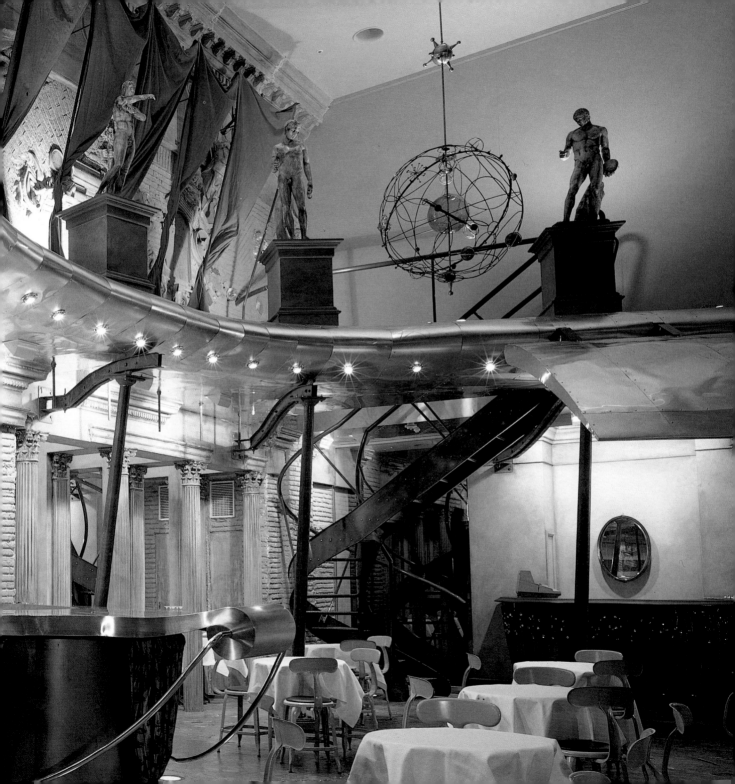

necessity. Land values in Tokyo were increasing with frightening rapidity. By mid-1987, plots of land in the centre of the city cost as much as £130,000 per square metre.[4] A commercial building needs to work very hard indeed to recoup that kind of investment. Ever since Kazumasa Yamashita stuck eyes, a nose and a mouth on one of his buildings in 1973, younger Japanese pop architects have been prepared to make a spectacle of their buildings. Many of the buildings of the 1980s are more adult but no less strident in their desire to make passers-by stop in their tracks. And since the primary function of a commercial building housing shops, bars or restaurants is to act as a form of three-dimensional advertising for the product inside, its days are very likely numbered from the start.

In the late 1980s, albeit in the face of considerable resistance from older, more conventional Japanese architects, the idea of the disposable building, with perhaps a ten-year lifespan, is gaining ground. The Japanese have, in any case, never been very ardent about preserving buildings, as the fate of Frank Lloyd Wright's Imperial Hotel, demolished in 1967, notoriously shows. Among the new guard there are even architects, such as Ke'iche Irie, who welcome the fluidity of the

54

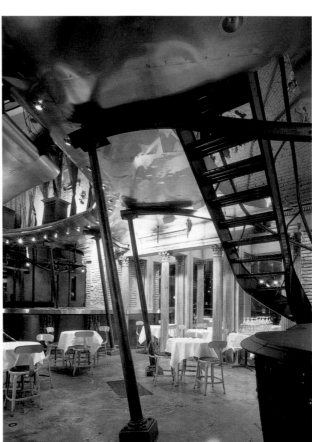

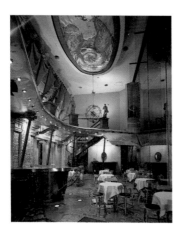

Above, tilting, cast-iron Victorian columns, shipped over from England, support the aluminium balcony. Left, a ceiling painting by Adam Lowe occupies an elliptical void

contemporary city and positively celebrate the fact "that Tokyo is like a computer program which ceaselessly keeps adding new subroutines. Western language itself, and your aspirations for buildings – which both emphasise order and clarity – seem now, to us, to be like a straitjacket. We don't believe in moulding life to the straight lines of an ideal building."[5]

As an outsider, Coates, too, has spoken of this "extraordinary sense of the city breaking apart and reforming, like gas".[6] And precisely because he is an outsider he has played a part in the process. For decades, with only a handful of exceptions, Japan was closed to foreign architects. The way Japanese construction companies and developers did business prevented foreigners from working there and the cost of bringing in architects from abroad was in any case prohibitive. Since the mid-1980s, though, the value of the yen has soared against the dollar, making the fees charged by overseas architects much closer to those for homegrown talent. At the same time, the vast increase in land prices means that construction costs are a much smaller proportion of the total investment in a new building. One obvious way to increase the value of the investment is to increase the value of the architecture; and the way to do that is to put up a building or design an interior so extraordinary that no magazine in town wants to lose such a photo-opportunity. Using an occidental superstar not only increases the likelihood of crowd-pulling publicity, but adds an extra dimension of authenticity (as at the Metropole) that the Japanese feel only the West can supply. As Coates has noted: "We seem to have something which people want and which curiously enough Japanese designers don't seem to be able to do.... They don't have the same way of handling architectural elements, particularly classical ones, that we do. In Europe there's a cultivated individuality which the Japanese have recently cottoned on to."[7] And if developers are very astute in their choices of site, the value of the surrounding land may even rise as well – particularly convenient if they happen to own it already.

Coates was one of the first, with Norman Foster and Philippe Starck, in a trickle of Western designers and architects that has become a well-documented flood. Richard Rogers, Michael Graves, Frank Gehry, Stanley Tigerman, Aldo Rossi, Mario Botta, Peter Eisenman, Zaha Hadid, Jean-Michel Wilmotte and David Chipperfield are just some of the designers who have either completed Japanese projects or are presently

55

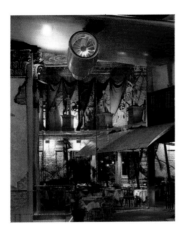

The wing-flap entrance canopy appears to penetrate the window, relating the inside to the outside and the lower space to the upper

working on them. Coates, a virtual novice when he arrived in Tokyo, is almost alone, however, in having produced designs which are a response to Japan so specialised that he could probably never have found a use for them anywhere else.

To people bemused by the apparent aggression of the aircraft wing he jammed into the front of the Caffè Bongo, Coates is fond of pointing out how loud the rest of the street is. The mass of the Parco department store weighs down on the corner unit which houses the café; the area is a riot of attractions competing for the shoppers who surge along the street. All the major department stores have bases in this part of Shibuya. Round the corner from Parco is Atsushi Kitagawara's Rise building, a shop/theatre/cinema complex, with a roof draped over it like molten curtains. Undue aesthetic modesty in this neighbourhood is an infallible way of being ignored. So, where the narrative content of the Metropole was subtle, something that had to be teased out and might well go overlooked, in Caffè Bongo it is eye-slammingly explicit. No one could mistake Bongo's superimpositions for anywhere that had ever existed. Coates fuses Piranesian Rome with 1950s "Espresso Modern" and binds the whole thing with an overlay of up-to-the-minute salvage.

The aircraft wing and jet engines outside, crowning a chipped Corinthian column, signal the aeronautical excesses to come. As you enter, a riveted aluminium balcony like an aircraft wing swings overhead, turning the L-shaped space into an auditorium, whose stage, on the other side of the plate-glass window, is the street. The walls are a crumbling collage of historical fragments and twentieth-century junk (an electric fan, a saw, some tongs and the dangling receiver of a phone). There are weird tilting columns, homoerotic statues on pedestals and classical mouldings. The floor is embedded with spanners, nuts, a padlock, a hinge and fragments of mosaic that suggest an archaeology of the present, given a camp twist by video screens bedded in floor-level fissures, playing Fellini's *La Dolce Vita* in a never-ending loop (they have since been removed). As with the Metropole, Coates commissioned a team of London artists and craftspeople, including Ron O'Donnell, David Phillips, Adam Lowe and André Dubreuil, to help give his fantasies substance.

Caffè Bongo perhaps lacks that sense of spatial dynamism that Coates's drawings so beautifully imply. It is a spectacle for gazing into more than for moving around. Unless you are directly under the wing balcony,

56

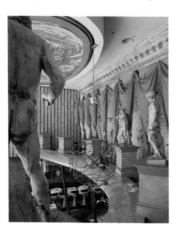

Tarnished classical statues, left, preside over the café. Opposite left, ground-floor plan of the Caffè Bongo, showing the prow of the bar. Opposite right, first-floor plan, showing the external wing

following the curve, it seems to push you away rather than draw you on, despite the use of devices such as a bar with a ship-like prow to signify movement. Parco's management hasn't helped by closing Coates's original street entrance, tucked under the wing flap that penetrates the window. Instead, they have opened up two side entrances inside the main building, neither of which leads so satisfactorily into the space. Even for the sensation-saturated Japanese, Caffè Bongo's imagery seems pitched at a level of excitement way beyond the needs of the café's simple programme. This is why suggestions that the café is the most NATO-esque of all Coates's completed projects are only half right. NATO's scrambled signs were always intended as spurs to action. Their get-up-and-go narratives assumed levels of interaction and participation simply not possible in a setting where nothing more provocative happens than the taking of afternoon tea. NATO might have livened the place up, on paper at least, by putting a launderette or a car wash in the corner.

In terms of its narrative layering, though, Caffè Bongo does many of the things NATO's city projects seemed to promise. As Coates has often said, Tokyo itself "already looks and works like a NATO city. It's got the reuse

misuse (sic), the layers, the distortions, the gaps and the chances... not, as in London, because of a collective breakdown, but because life works and holds together that way."[8] One might even say that Caffè Bongo embodies the "imprint of one reality on another" that Coates had savoured in cities everywhere and found in Tokyo in abundance. In Tokyo, three-tier highways snake through a patchwork city organised according to no determinable logic, forever skirting a centre, the grounds of the Imperial Palace, which is mysteriously absent. Buildings clamour to be heard above their neighbours; zoning restrictions don't appear to exist. People wearing American-style kit play baseball in a wooded ground among the warehouses and factories, while washing dries on the balconies of the nearby apartment blocks and logs float down the river in the direction of a paper mill. Love hotels with towers and turrets like enchanted castles cluster at the intersections where the highways merge. In Akihabara, the world's most advanced electronic consumer goods are sold in a glorified street market. In Shinjuku, the *Blade Runner* buildings act as giant neon signs blinking to the rhythms of the city while salarymen eat noodles in the shanty town of restaurants next to the Yamanote line as the trains trundle overhead.

57

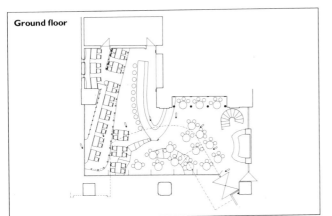

Ground floor

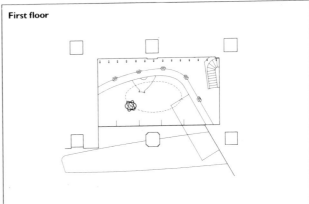

First floor

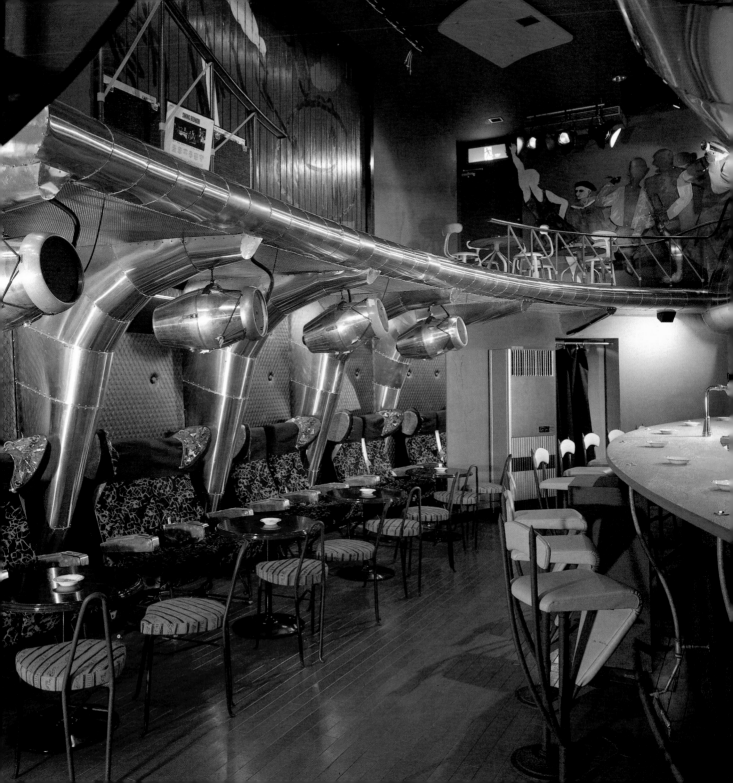

"Harness the city-scape as it is and take it even further," wrote Coates and NATO. "It'll happen anyhow. If architects don't do it others will."[9] Perhaps he was thinking of the problems he had experienced with his third Tokyo project, for the Takeo Kikuchi building designed by Tadao Ando, Japanese heir to the modernism of Le Corbusier, Mies van der Rohe and Louis Kahn. The 1986 project suggested, more acutely perhaps than any previous project in Tokyo, that conventional minimalism and 1980s maximalism are on a collision course. Where Coates has attempted to capture the signs of the city, twist them and reflect them back in his designs, Ando and others like him react to urban chaos with an architecture of uncompromising visual purity. Ando's buildings might not harmonise with their surroundings (how could they when their surroundings are so crass?), but at least within their walls the architect can banish the ephemeral and trashy, and impose a restraint impossible in the city outside.

Takeo Kikuchi, fashion designer and jazz fan, asked Coates to create three interiors for the building: a double-height basement jazz club, the Bohemia; a ground-floor shop, selling Kikuchi's menswear; and a first-floor barber's shop. Shi Yu Chen acted once again as

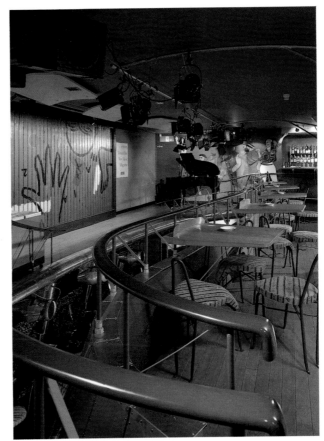

59

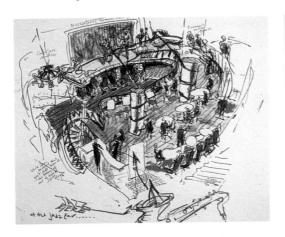

Opposite and above, the basement bar at the Bohemia jazz club was Coates's second exercise in crashed-wing aesthetics. Salvaged aircraft seats occupy alcoves formed by swollen aluminium fins. Left, X-ray drawing by Coates

producer on the project. Bohemia is the most successful of these spaces and in many ways the most satisfying of Coates's trio of Tokyo projects. It is his own favourite too. It saw Coates continuing to play with aircraft imagery, but discarding the classical imagery that had been such a strong feature of the Metropole and Caffè Bongo. His aim with Bohemia, he said, was to evoke the atmosphere of "a grubby little *boîte*, or a Soho clipjoint from the 1950s";[10] the club is an idealised, more than slightly souped-up version of what such a beatnik jazz hang-out might have been like. Its conviction comes in large measure from its very off-handedness. Coates's by now familiar method of drafting in a team of artist and artisan contributors (here NATO members Mark Prizeman and Catrina Beevor, and painter Bruce McLean) has given Bohemia the air of having developed gradually over time, rather than being designed in a rush. The entrance is on the top floor, so that coming in you can look down into the space. A bulging, aluminium-clad balcony twists away towards the end wall and doubles back as a Bongo-like wing along the other side to form a makeshift aerial platform for visiting jazz bands. A spiral staircase leads down past Coates's chandelier made out of miniature plastic saxophones to the lower bar, where

there is a line of salvaged aircraft seats in alcoves formed by bloated aluminium fins. Jet-engine conga drums by Peter Thomas and Peter Sabara, originally intended to contain fans, hang above each of the tables. The space is theatrical yet functional in the way it encourages circulation, with an intimacy, despite the turbocharged baroque, quite lacking in Caffè Bongo.

Coates and Kikuchi originally talked about the possibility of recasting Ando's concrete building as a London house. They can hardly have been surprised that Ando wasn't keen. In fact, Ando wasn't very keen on any of Coates's proposed additions to the exterior. The plan of the building is trapeziform with a curved-wall core, creating a roofless "zen courtyard" (in actuality a dingy staircase) between the core and the rear external wall. It was here that Coates wanted to install a "drainpipe" sculpture. His request was politely declined. The problem arose again at the front. To mark the entrance, Coates wanted to attach a barber's pole, two welded steel candelabra by Tom Dixon and a pair of fluorescent signs. Once again Ando politely but firmly declined. He didn't want any electrical illumination fixed to the wall; he didn't want anything fixed to the wall. In the end, amid some bad feeling, Coates managed the barber's pole, one

Bohemia's balcony seating area and platform for visiting musicians frames the curve of the bar counter below

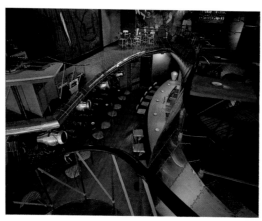

Ground floor (menswear shop)

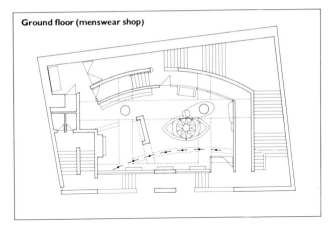

First floor (barber's shop)

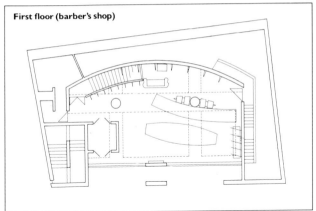

Basement (Bohemia)

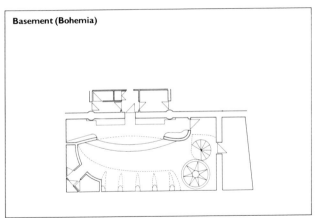

Upper basement (Bohemia)

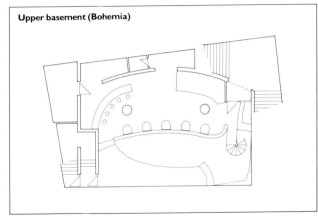

61

*Floorplans of the
Bohemia jazz club,
menswear shop and
barber's in the
Takeo Kikuchi
building*

candelabrum and a single pink neon sign saying
"Bohemia".

Inside the menswear shop, Coates and Kikuchi were
able to pursue their regressive fantasies of the English
country house and public school more or less unhindered.
Antlers are roped to salvaged columns shipped over from
London and a stuffed fox stands in the recycled fireplace.
There are animal heads, cricket bats, sporting trophies,
fat leather armchairs, displays of mounted butterflies and
sturdy suitcases full of shirts that suggest a weekend in
the country. The changing room is a schoolboy's bedroom
scattered with books and games. Carlos Villanueva has
fashioned a lectern out of wriggling wire and Robert
Mull has made standard lamps from sandbags. On the
floor above, in the barber's shop, André Dubreuil has
constructed a chandelier and there is a ceiling painting by
Adam Lowe. The result is a set piece of simulated
Victoriana made all the more bizarre by the austerity of
its container. But, as Coates himself has pointed out, it is
not without sensitivity to Ando's spaces: "Although the
vocabulary we executed in that building was very
different from Ando's, we did try to think about the
forms of the building and how to allow them to progress
into another vocabulary. For instance the curve of the

columns in the shop is not exactly parallel to the curved
wall of the space, but it's suggesting that there's another
geometry hidden inside the one of his building. We built
all those curved corners and I think it was carefully done
to make some use of the form of the building."[11]

That may be so, but the oppositions embodied in the
Takeo Kikuchi building are thrown into even more
dramatic relief by the building Coates has designed for a
plot opposite Ando's on the other side of the road. This
time, too, the situation is reversed; the five-storey
building is Coates's, but someone else will take charge of
the interiors. The Wall, as Coates calls it, sees a return to
some of the imagery and themes of Caffè Bongo – and not
simply in the inverted aircraft undercarriage wheels that
have been cast in bronze for the cornice. In The Wall, the
immediate future is superimposed on the past to form an
analogue of the city itself (Tokyo has twice been destroyed
and rebuilt this century, as the result first of earthquake
then of war). As the building rose in the summer of
1989, a hoarding with a giant handwritten message
announced its intentions to the street: "The concept for
the building revolves around a wall of monumental
proportions – a wall which could have been built by the
Romans, a wall of stone and giant arches, a wall which

62

For the Takeo Kikuchi menswear shop, right, Coates introduced the eccentric bric-à-brac of an English country house into a concrete building by Tadao Ando that could not have been more severe

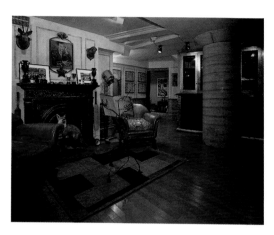 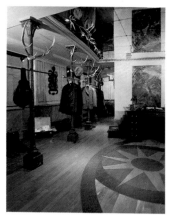

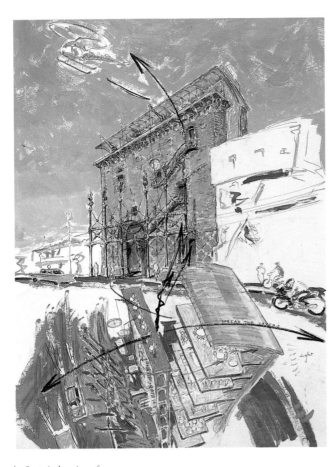

Coates's drawing of The Wall in Nishi Azabu, Tokyo, on a site across the road from the Takeo Kikuchi building. All the building's main architectural events are concentrated at the front between the cast-iron frame and the facade

could have encircled cities. But unlike the ruins of Rome, this wall is both ancient and still being built. Atop its giant cornices, blocks of stone lie waiting to be placed. Sculptures in the form of ancient building cranes suggest that the building is continuing to grow, towards the future into the 21st century."[12] A cast-iron frame, like a flattened Victorian gasometer, forms a zone of passage between the "archaeological" facade and the street, adding another layer to Coates's historical collage. The orientation of the building is, more than anything, televisual. Everything happens at the front and is projected forwards through the frame into the street. The staircases weaving in and out of the facade turn visitors into characters in the architectural drama.

Audacious even by Tokyo standards, The Wall is another collaboration with Shi Yu Chen, now styling himself as "driving force" rather than producer. Without Chen's intercessions it is almost impossible to imagine how such a project could have come about. No client, however broad-minded in his search for novelty, is going to ask for a building like this. On the other hand, as Coates was at pains to point out, he wasn't given carte blanche to be as crazy as he liked. The projects weren't confidence tricks being perpetrated on naive clients with

63

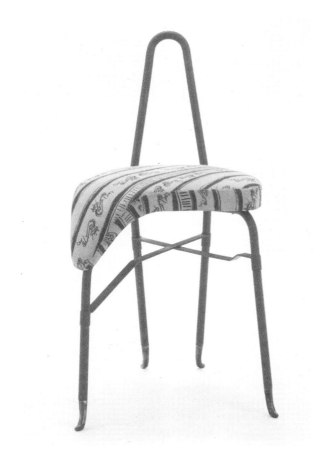

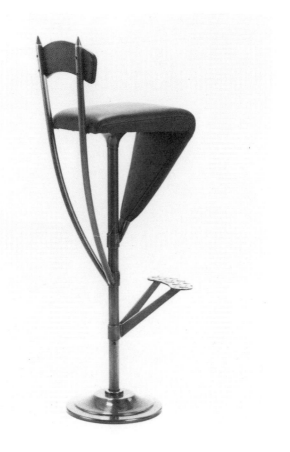

64

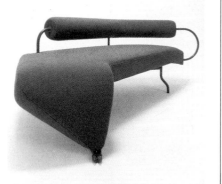

The Japanese
furniture company
Rockstone has
introduced a
number of richly
detailed pieces by
Coates. Above, the
Jazz chair and Jazz
bar stool, both
originally designed
for Bohemia. Left,
the Shoes sofa

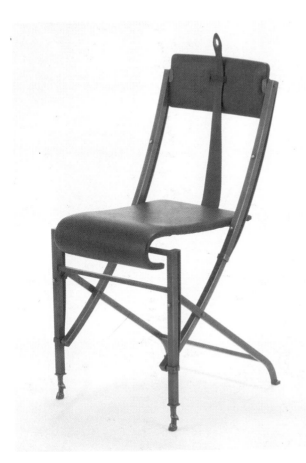

too much money and too little taste. The Japanese might not have been able to imagine what they were getting in advance, they might not have understood it fully when they got it, but they knew exactly why they needed it. Branson Coates were given the go-ahead because their proposals were perceived to make commercial sense. It was Coates's exceptional good fortune that the Japanese taste for fusing the ancient and ultra-modern happened to coincide with his own avant-garde interests. Once they had taken him up, there seemed to be no limit to the opportunities they were prepared to supply. In 1987, the Tokyo furniture company, Rockstone, put into production thirteen of Coates's designs for the Metropole and Takeo Kikuchi projects, including the Horse side chair and the Jazz bar stool. Even by Milanese standards it was a spectacularly confident debut. In an entrepreneurial climate where the unpredictable happens as a matter of routine, Coates and Chen have since been consulted on designs for sunglasses, hand-luggage and a range of work clothes.

Coates hasn't had everything his own way, though: a commercial building for the city of Ashiya, a promising, Gaudi-esque vision of towers and watery cascades, was cancelled after the developer decided he could make more 65

The Dog chair, above, also for Rockstone, collapses when pulled by its backrest strap. Right, the bar stool and Chariot armchair, both created for the Metropole. All three pieces have animal-like feet

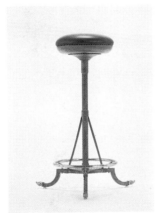
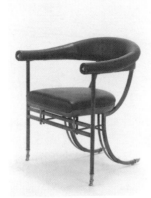

money by selling the site. Even more frustrating, one suspects, are the changes clients have made to completed projects. All have suffered to some degree, but none more grievously than the Caffè Bongo. Its owner, Parco, has shortened the bar to make more room for tables, changed the chairs because they were thought to be uncomfortable, removed the *Dolce Vita* videos, which it never understood, altered the entrance in an attempt to increase custom, and replaced the external wing by a plastic replica. Coates is philosophical about this: "Quite honestly I didn't expect it to last as long as it did!"[13] Chen now reckons on a project's lasting two years before it begins to "decay" like Bongo, or gets stripped out and replaced.

Buildings appear to offer more permanence, even if "permanence" turns out to be only a decade or so. Coates's first completed building, L'Arca di Noè (Noah's Ark), a restaurant and bar in the city of Sapporo on the island of Hokkaido, could not be much more solid. The developer, Jasmac, owner of a number of other hotel and leisure developments in the area, wanted a "shining jewel" for the riverside site. In theory, five storeys were available to Coates, but he needed just two to make an architectural statement stranger than anything else built by a British

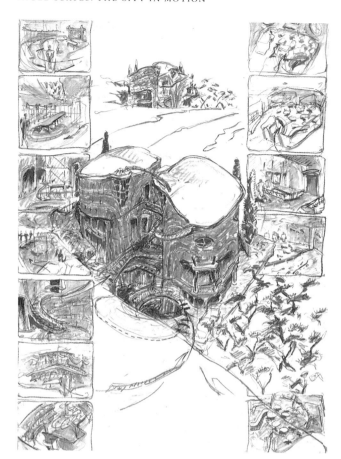

Coates's unbuilt design for a commercial building in Ashiya was inspired by the drums, pipes and conveyors of a cement works. Its organic forms recall the work of Gaudi

architect in the last twenty years. L'Arca di Noè belongs to no recognisable contemporary school, though it certainly qualifies for inclusion in the annals of fantastic or bizarre architecture alongside such oddities as the Palais Idéal of Ferdinand Cheval, or Rudolf Steiner's organic-roofed boilerhouse of 1914-1915.[14] One might call it a folly except that it has a function, which it fulfils very smoothly. Coates himself sees the Ark as one of a kind, a "pavilion of sensations" created for unusual conditions, in which he was able to concentrate a density of effect he could hardly expect to repeat elsewhere. His aim, he said, was to design a building that would transport the imagination as well as the body. Photographs make the building look rather a monster, lumbering forward like a three-legged elephant. Yet its presence, softened by a line of willow trees and the riverside setting, is surprisingly gentle. L'Arca di Noè was only completed in October 1988, but it already looks as though it has been there for years. The quality of the workmanship, particularly in the wooden fittings, is very high, reinforcing an impression of permanence and history.

The building's simple representational conceit is that of Noah's Ark run aground on a mountain – Fuji rather

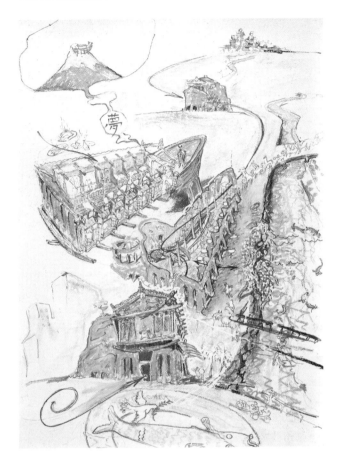

Multiple viewpoint drawing by Coates of the Arca di Noè restaurant on the island of Hokkaido. In a thought bubble at the top of the image, the building appears to be dreaming of its origins as an Ark

67

than Ararat, Coates has said. However arbitrary it might seem, the narrative idea was primarily a response to the limitations of a narrow, triangular site. The client's original suggestion of a temple, for instance, could never have worked. On one side, the prow emerges from a formless mass of rock (concrete sprayed on to nets) housing kitchens and services; on the other, windows lean out over the river like the stern of a pirate galleon. The upper storey and roof are Etruscan in style; inside, plaster finishes with the texture of sandstone are remarkably effective in suggesting a petrified wooden structure. Despite the heavy post and lintel construction, the effect in the daytime is light and open. Spatially, the building is the most sophisticated of Coates's projects to date, a sustained attempt to apply his thinking of the 1970s about gardens and theatres to an enclosed architectural space. Entrances at the prow and stern increase the flow of customers and solicit a desire to explore the building, turning the visitor from passive onlooker into an active participant required to make choices. The theatricality of the ground-floor bar is emphasised by the use of non-structural columns to form a sequence of sectional slices resembling the wings of a stage. By directing attention to the windows while breaking up the plane of

the wall, the columns help to engage the building with the river outside (upstairs the leaning windows and dipping external canopies perform a similar function). The hull-like curved beams that cross the central "keel" of the Ark not only amplify these rhythms, but serve to relate the lower structure to that of the restaurant above. Originally, it was planned that a wooden staircase would run up the outside of the building, but the client wanted to fill in as much of the site's volume as possible. Instead, a staircase like a ship's gangway, or the ramp of the original Ark, runs in a straight line from the prow door to the top-floor restaurant, where it collides unexpectedly with a second, more conventionally palatial spiral staircase serving the other entrance. This, the building's single most impressive spatial moment, is the point at which its alternative channels of movement are consummated and resolved.

Fittingly, the Ark's iconographic programme also reaches a climax here in a stairwell fresco by Stuart Helm, depicting exotic plant forms and Noah's chosen animals in a mystical dance. Works of art and objects on the theme of the Ark are placed throughout in such a way as to emphasise the dialogue between the building and its site or, as in the fresco, to underscore the mechanics of

68

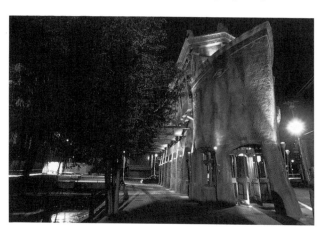

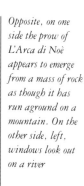

Opposite, on one side the prow of L'Arca di Noè appears to emerge from a mass of rock as though it has run aground on a mountain. On the other side, left, windows look out on a river

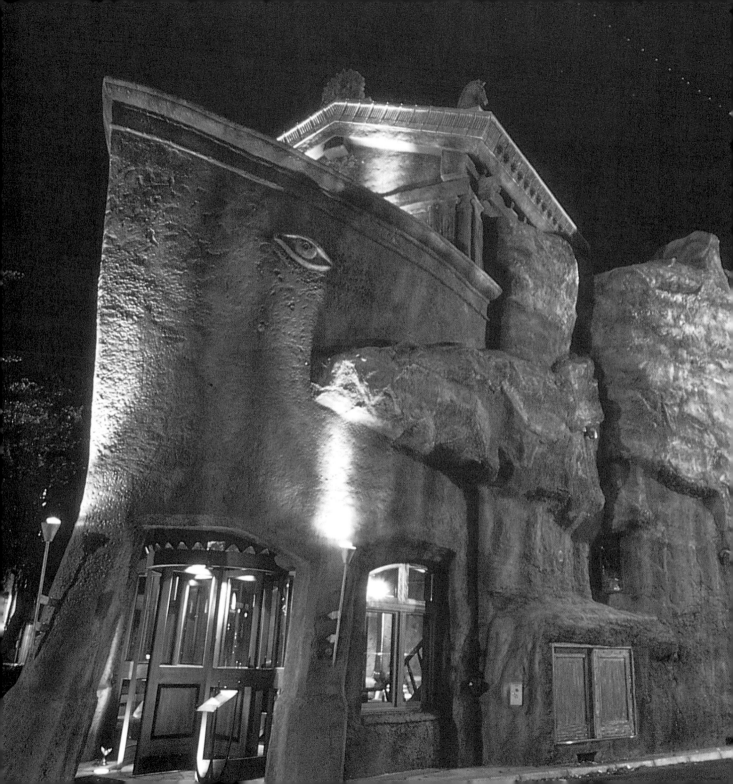

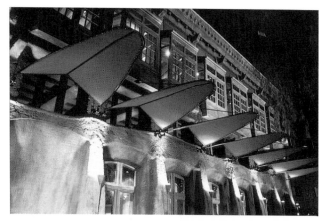

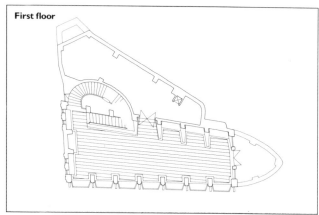

First floor

70

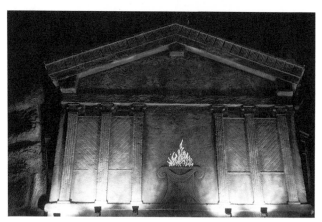

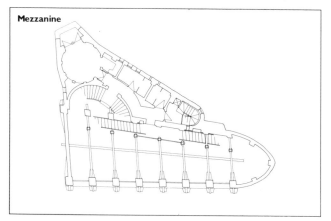

Mezzanine

Top left, oar-like canopies help to relate the Ark to the river. Above, the "stern" elevation features a flickering fibre optic brazier. Right, the building's triangular plan arises from the constraints of its site

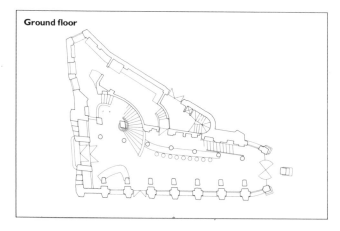

Ground floor

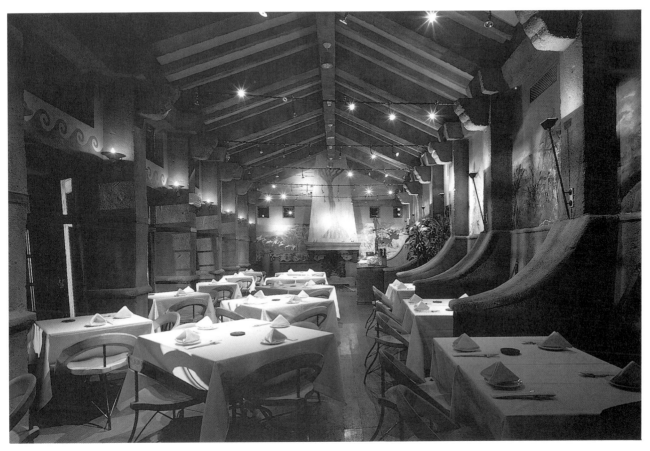

71

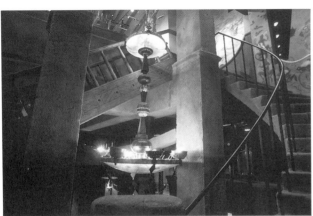

Inside, the building resembles a petrified wooden structure. Above, the upstairs restaurant, with chairs by Coates. Left, the meeting of the two staircases. Right, the ground-floor bar

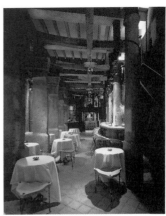

the space. They include frescoes by Adam Lowe, wall hangings by Annabel Grey, vases by Beverly Beeland, a chandelier by Tom Dixon and a junkyard sculpture by Marc Quinn, which stands on the prow. The stools and chairs designed by Coates in sandblasted and oiled ash and steel have a similar elemental quality and a sense of almost muscular tension (three pieces were launched as the Noah collection by the London company SCP at the Milan Furniture Fair in 1988).

L'Arca di Noè is too personal and wayward to be written off simply as an exercise in Etruscan theming. It answers a commercial need – the regeneration of a seedy downtown neighbourhood – but does so on its own defiant terms. Construction costs were twice as high as usual for a Japanese building of this size. Expensive effects such as the rock face were achieved only by trial and error. It took unusual conviction from both architect and producer to win the support of a nervous client and sceptical construction people. Such uncompromising attention to detail combines with the layers of allusion to give the building a dimension of pure play that brings it as close to art as to architecture. L'Arca di Noè, in many ways, is a sculpture for eating in.

With two extraordinary Japanese buildings and a large-scale hotel conversion in Otaru (1989) under his belt, Coates has confounded his critics and proved that his peculiar visions can be realised. But can they be built only under the conditions of freedom granted by the Japanese, or will he be able to translate his sensibility into an architecture acceptable to more conservative Western taste without blunting its essential power? His British projects suggest that, given the chance, he might.

72

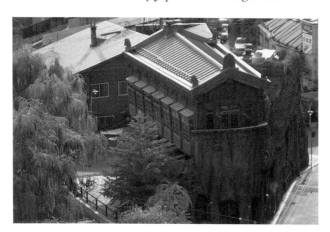

Aerial view of the Ark, left, showing its Etruscan-style upper storey. Opposite, Coates's exploded view of the Otaru Marittimo hotel in a converted bank building. Each of its rooms is based on one of the great ports of the world

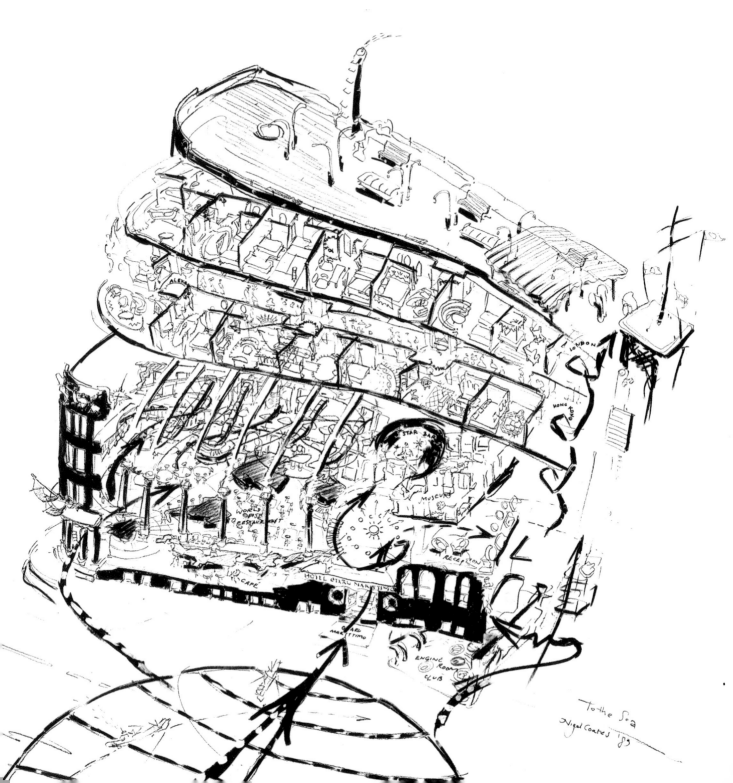

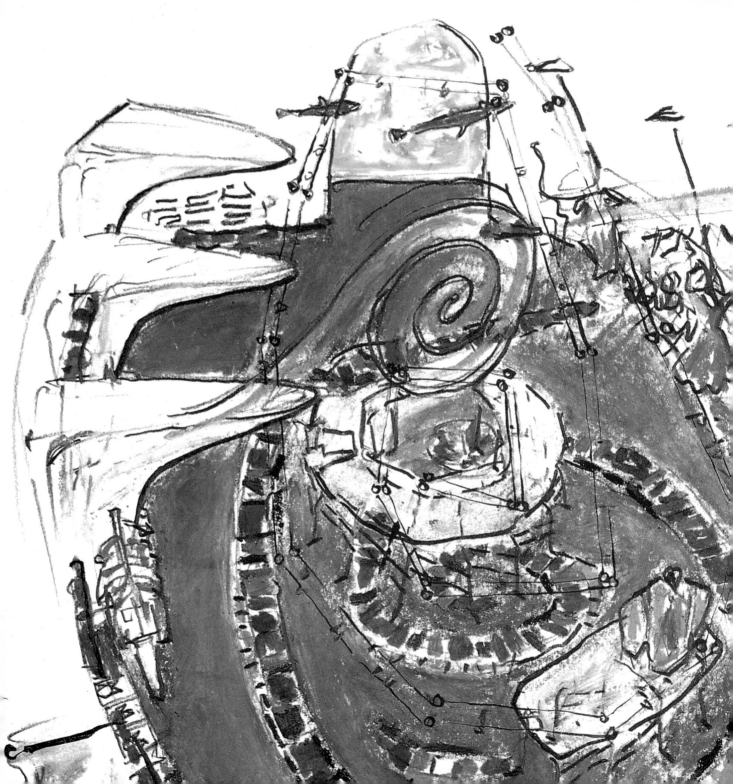

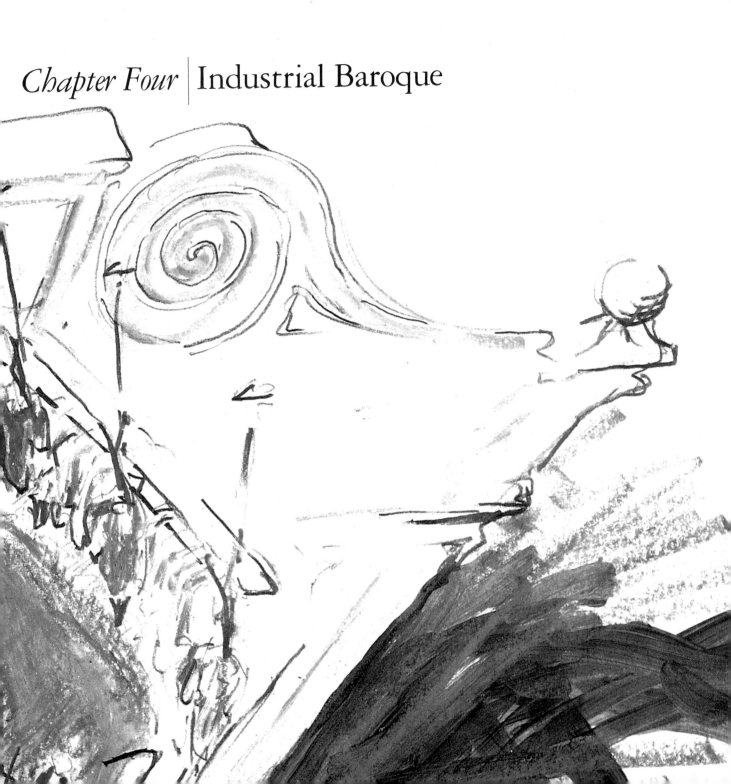

Chapter Four | Industrial Baroque

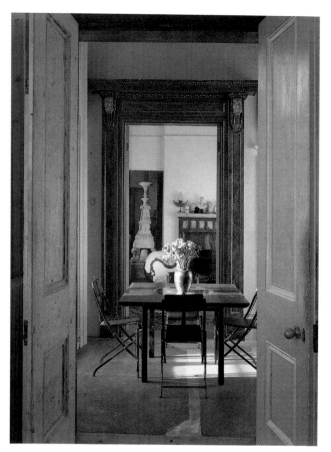

Nigel Coates's Japanese projects have been created in a climate and a culture (some would say an absence of culture) where anything is possible. For the time being at least, no fantasy is too bizarre or improbable for Japanese taste, or too expensive for the Japanese budget. If Coates had not been invited to design there, it is hard to see how his career could have developed with anything like the same momentum. Philippe Starck, who arrived in Tokyo at much the same time, had a satchelful of *causes célèbres* to his credit, from the Elysée Palace to the Café Costes; Coates had a portfolio of provocative theories and a particularly striking flat. As a result, Japan has acted as a testbed for ideas so outrageous by British standards that they could almost certainly never have risen from the drawing board had he remained in London. Yet the photographs of these unreachable projects published so widely in Western magazines were proof that his fantasies could, after all, be built. They confirmed Coates as a designer of unusual daring and imagination, at least when it came to small-scale commercial projects such as restaurants, cafés and clubs, and they conferred on him a kind of dangerous glamour. Coates, the AA outsider, had cracked it. He had travelled to the city at the end of the world (a place as exotic to European eyes in the 1980s as

Previous page, detail of Coates's drawing of Katharine Hamnett's Glasgow shop. Above and opposite, Coates's London flat: stripped doors, marbled doorways and an air of decay that captivated the Japanese

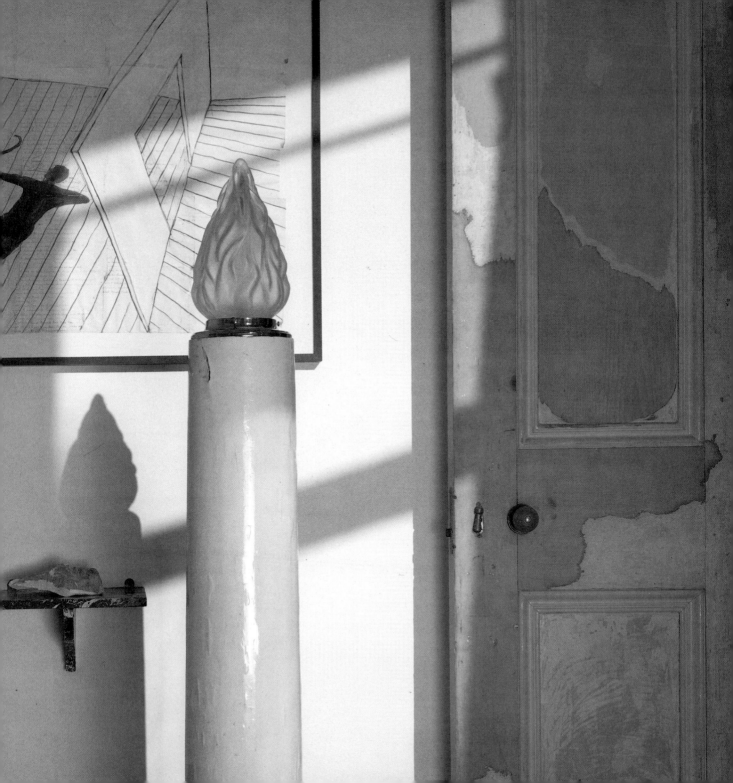

America in the 1950s), fathomed the desires of the mysterious Japanese, and pulled off a series of projects that turned him virtually overnight into a celebrity of sorts.

Clearly, however, this was not a designer for the faint-hearted; in Britain, it was mainly fashion designers and people from the more luxurious end of retailing who gravitated towards Coates, clients sufficiently close in spirit to take a chance on his experimentalism. The most surprising thing about these British projects, to anyone anticipating the collage excesses of Tokyo, is their restraint. But it is this very restraint and sensitivity to context that lend credence to Coates's claims that he is using a method and not brushing on a style.

Branson Coates's first British commercial project, completed in the summer of 1986, was a shop for the fashion designer Jasper Conran in Beauchamp Place, the Knightsbridge fashion enclave. Before starting the practice, Coates had worked on Conran's house in Regent's Park, a straightforward if technically awkward conversion involving a certain amount of structural alteration. The finished interior was understated and discreet, occasionally budding into flamboyance — as in the eighteenth-century grey stone fireplaces and the

78

Coates's first project before forming Branson Coates Architecture was a Regent's Park house conversion for the fashion designer Jasper Conran

Genoese chandelier that hung above the dining table. "Jasper forced me to mix my interest in narrative and fluid spaces with a previously absent restraint; I learned to use less than I thought was needed," Coates said later.[1] At Conran's request, the shop was a continuation of this intimate, homely aesthetic, and it does feel like a town house as much as a space for retailing. Bare oak boards fixed by dowels are used throughout and the specially made oak cabinets also have a domestic air. The easy flow of spaces is nicely expressed by a sinuous balustrade with a beech and brass rail, which courses downstairs to the basement. Here and upstairs, the hanging system has a double function, erupting in brass torch-like light-fittings. The only real concession to theatricality in this understated shop is a row of tiny footlights in the window, which converts the facade into a proscenium and the shoppers into players.

Coates has described the project as a kind of "minimalist baroque"; the "baroque" part, at least, is a term that has stuck. In August 1986, two of his drawings, one of them for the Jasper Conran shop, were included in an exhibition of "Designs for Interiors" at the Victoria and Albert Museum. The exhibition classified contemporary decorators' styles according to six categories: Classical and Neo-Classical; Grand Luxe; Moderne; Haut Décor; Post-Modern; and New Baroque. Coates was grouped among the latter with David Connor, Tom Dixon, André Dubreuil, Oriel Harwood, Ron Arad and others. What linked these designers, according to the exhibition's organiser, Stephen Calloway, was a shared admiration for what the painter John Piper once called "pleasing decay". Possible sources included the imagery of Cecil Beaton, the tastes of the literary Sitwells, the war-time neo-romantic artists (such as Piper) and "visually obsessive" film-makers such as Fellini and Derek Jarman (both undoubtedly influences in Coates's case). "As if in reaction to the complacency of much interior decoration and stirred by a perversely romantic attitude to urban wreckage a number of young designers seem either independently or in small groups to have arrived at a curiously obscure but exciting and expressive neo-baroque aesthetic," wrote Calloway.[2] The essence of the style, he concluded in a phrase that might have been coined for the Caffè Bongo, was "grandeur and a new theatricality: the *mise-en-scène* a ruined palazzo in a post-holocaust landscape".

The other Coates drawing included in the exhibition was for the Silver jewellery shop in London, which opened   79

Jasper Conran's shop in Beauchamp Place, Knightsbridge. Coates's fluid, X-ray style of drawing explains the space by tugging it apart at the seams

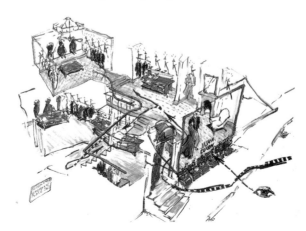

in 1987. Silver was a more florid application of the same principles, but its imagery was "industrial" where the Jasper Conran shop's was minimal; Coates himself dubbed it an example of "industrial baroque". "Industrial baroque is about process and movement. It has a certain theatricality and excessiveness and, like baroque, appreciates plant-like forms. I see a lot of these qualities in machinery."[3] As with the Conran shop and the Japanese projects, the Silver interior was represented in Coates's drawing as an exploded perspective view, as though the outside walls and internal structure had become suddenly transparent and only the spaces remained. This is Coates's so-called "X-ray" style and it has proved to be his favourite tool for describing circulation, revealing the way in which spaces relate and elaborating their drama. He explains: "In the initial stages I try to visualise the building as a place after it is built. I think of the people in it and the way they will look at it – find the sources in that. I use the sketchbook as a catalyst. I love the irrationality of drawing – just to draw a line and see what happens. It's not quite automatic drawing, but it's starting with something you know, such as the outline of a site. You draw it and very often it develops into something else and it's that

development which you can't do simply by sitting down and analysing something and redrawing it using the usual logical processes of design. I much prefer a process which uses sequential operations to allow the unpredictable element to emerge. It's a conversation between the mind and the paper."[4]

In the finished drawings, long, swirling arrows and loose, fluid lines imbue the image with a sense of movement. The arrows indicate the user's most likely route and encourage the viewer to explore the spaces imaginatively in a way that does not always happen with more static representations. Sometimes, as with Silver, Coates draws a single human eye at the entrance to his spaces, switching the emphasis from the formal intentions of the drawing to the nature of the perceiver's experience. In more elaborate drawings, such as the one for L'Arca di Noè, he presents a montage of viewpoints (perhaps analogous to a much simplified cubism) which seek to convey the totality of the structure in a single image. The same is true of Coates's drawing for Silver. Details of the corner shop's canopies and displays are extracted, lifted, tilted and superimposed on the base image to form a composite impression of the main design elements.

80

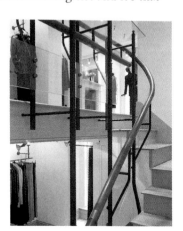

Detail of the beech and brass stair rail that forms a centrepiece at the otherwise restrained Jasper Conran shop

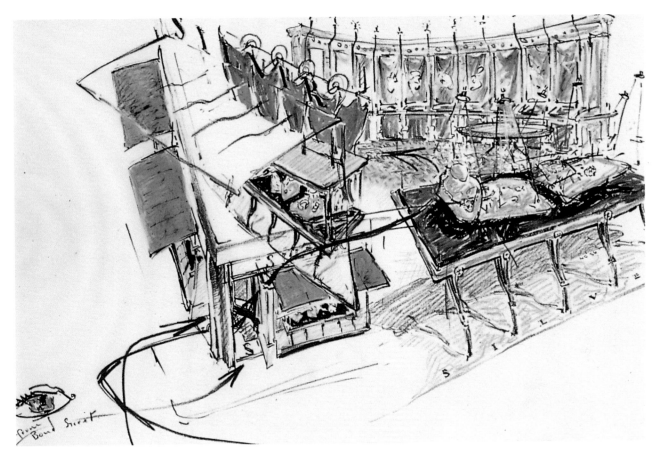

*Coates's drawing of
the Silver jewellery
shop. The corner
was cut back
behind the column
to form a curved
entrance that
found a visual echo
in the curved
display cases at the
back*

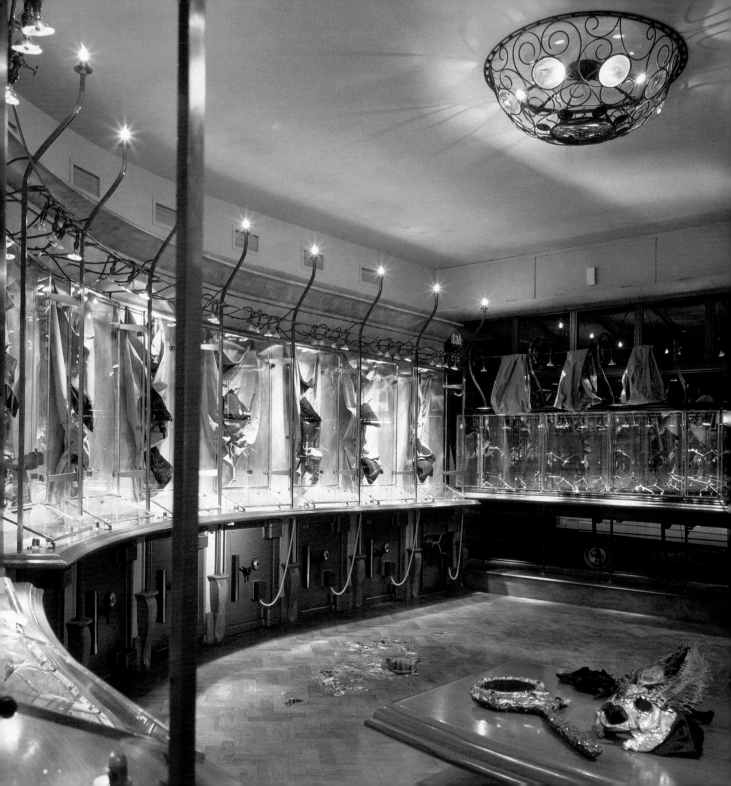

Of all Coates's British projects, Silver is the one with the greatest air of durability. The clients, Bernard Silver and his son Nicholas, specialise in "art" jewellery, from historical originals to the taxidermy trinkets of Simon Costin. They had seen pictures of the Metropole restaurant in a magazine and asked Coates for a design with the same elegance and expressive use of metalwork as Fouquet, a turn-of-the-century jewellers in Paris. But the 1960s plate-glass and granite building they had chosen on the corner of Cork Street and Burlington Gardens seemed at first sight intractable. The windows had to be retained, making it that much harder to distinguish the shop from the rest of the building and to focus attention on objects at the intimate scale of jewellery. The solution Coates devised was both practical and semiotic. Wing-like canopies sprout from the facade, intensifying the colours below with their shade and drawing the eye to glass cabinets in which the jewellery is held up to view by a framework of laboratory clamps. The clamps are new rather than recycled (this is *bricolage* not salvage) and patinated to suggest a luxury not normally associated with the classroom world of bunsen burners, lab benches and chemicals in glass jars. At a stroke, they send up the essential pomposity of the enterprise while giving a knowing nudge to the avant-garde clientele Silver hopes to attract. A line of safes along the curved, freestanding wall at the back serves much the same purpose. Only four of them are real, the rest being a joke at the putative safe-breaker's expense. The notion of "value" is gently lampooned and upheld at the same time. The most baroque touches, apart from the clamps, are in the metalwork. Torch lights "like aircraft landing lights" (Coates),[5] brass curlicues interspersed with swags of blue silk and a chandelier by André Dubreuil fuse to create an interior suspended somewhere in the great divide between "traditional" and "modern" that Coates was rapidly making his own.

The Jasper Conran shop and Silver established Branson Coates as London designers able to supply upmarket clients with a timely alternative to minimalism or high tech. In 1988, the practice brought a similar, almost gentlemanly elegance to bear on the design of an exhibition for Dunhill International, shown at the Mall Galleries, London. It also undertook two projects for the fashion designer Katharine Hamnett, whose previous but shortlived shop, designed by Norman Foster in 1987, had been one of the most widely celebrated London shops of the decade. Foster had favoured the most awe-inspiring

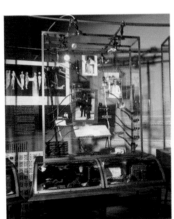

Opposite, Silver achieves a Parisian, turn-of-the-century glamour, but details such as the laboratory clamp display stands locate the project firmly in the 1980s. Right, a similar approach for the Dunhill exhibition

83

possible build-up – a long, curving entrance bridge leading to a vast converted garage, whose main embellishments were tall, space-extending mirrors. In turning to Coates, Hamnett, quixotic as ever, was moving about as far in the opposite aesthetic direction as it was possible to go. Their first project together was for a shop in Glasgow's Princes Square shopping centre in the heart of the city. Coates found it easy to achieve the rapport with Hamnett that he had always felt with fashion people and took her enthusiasm for Barcelona, Morocco and coloured tiles as a pointer. The project recalls no other architect so much as Gaudi, though admittedly a Gaudi purged of his more orchidaceous excesses. The small shop unit has been remodelled and replastered to turn it into a soft-walled cave, with a trio of curving buttresses to form bays for hanging clothes. A spiral of plain coloured tiles (green, orange, indigo and white) set into the terracotta floor emphasises the circularity of the space and is echoed by a ceiling light track which unwinds in the same direction. Further tiles follow the line of the display benches, which run along one wall. The only obviously perverse elements are the combination of fish tanks and video screens in the changing rooms, and the burnished metal "Katharine

Hamnett" sign, illuminated by three flashing light bulbs in the manner of a Soho clipjoint.

If the Glasgow shop saw Coates in relatively low gear, he more than made up for it with his second shop for Hamnett, which opened in Sloane Street, London in October 1988. This time, too, Hamnett had suggestions to make. Fish were still high on the list of priorities (Foster, reportedly, had banned them from the premises), so Coates has given pride of place in the window to a bank of steel-framed fish tanks decorated by Tom Dixon. (Not for Hamnett the cardinal retailers' rule that you must show the goods in the window. As with the Foster shop, and other more exclusive establishments before it, customers must make the effort to discover the merchandise.) Outside and in, the shop makes no secret of its theatrical intentions. The shopfront is framed by painted swags looping between torchères, and a curtain is drawn to one side as if to unveil the spectacle of selection and purchase. Beyond this notional proscenium are a number of exotic props meant to suggest the languorous pleasures of the salon (Beaton and Cocteau apparently provided the points of departure). A fake Venetian mirror, too big for its berth, towers above Coates's less ripe version of Dali's Mae West "lips" sofa, while an "exploded" Adam ceiling is framed by a lip of tubular cloth bound with chains. The mood is heightened by further fish tanks used to define and block off a rear corner, more swags of material (by Zaza Wentworth Stanley) and a light-fitting of cat's-cradle intricacy. Outside Japan, this is Coates's most incident-packed interior per square metre, but somehow the anticipated fusion of elements never quite occurs – and perhaps it was never meant to occur. More than any of Coates's other London projects this is a shop that seems hell-bent on proclaiming its own artificiality. Coates has described it as an exercise in "soft psychology" in contrast to "behaviourism".[6] At a time when retail design is developing ever more effective devices for inducing shoppers to part with their money, the Katharine Hamnett shop wears all its devices on its sleeve. The project is not an attempt to manipulate the shopper surreptitiously so much as a series of unconcealed invitations to climb on the stage and "play shopping". The desired result, it goes without saying, is the same in both cases.

Coates himself seems aware of the contradictions of his position and, of course, he is by no means the only architect to face them. They apply just as much to

Hamnett herself: how to reconcile populist inclinations, radical politics and exclusive prices? Wealthy clients catering to a wealthy audience have favoured Coates, but he would like his work to have a wider public. The earlier urban projects, however controversial they may have been, addressed the problems of a much broader spectrum of society. "One hopes that it isn't just the people who can afford these things who go there," Coates has said of the Hamnett shop in Sloane Street. "It is our long-term objective to make spaces which are not so exclusively related to particular privileged groups of people. I see our work as political and in each manifestation we've tried to make the most of what was possible without offending the client."[7]

In this respect, Coates's most interesting British projects of the 1980s are the shops he has designed for Jigsaw in London and Bristol – if only because they point the way out of the high fashion ghetto. Jigsaw is a small high-street fashion chain offering well-made clothes in natural fabrics for young women. They don't put their clothes on the catwalks of the big international fashion shows and their shops have never previously been noted for the quality of their design. On the surface, the match seemed unlikely, but Jigsaw had seen the Jasper Conran

85

Right and overleaf, decoration was kept to a minimum at Katharine Hamnett's Glasgow shop. A spiral of tiles set into the floor embodies the intended sense of movement in an essentially simple space

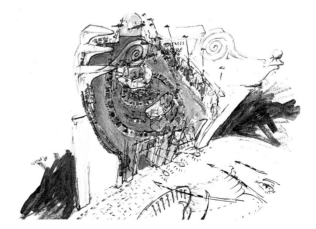

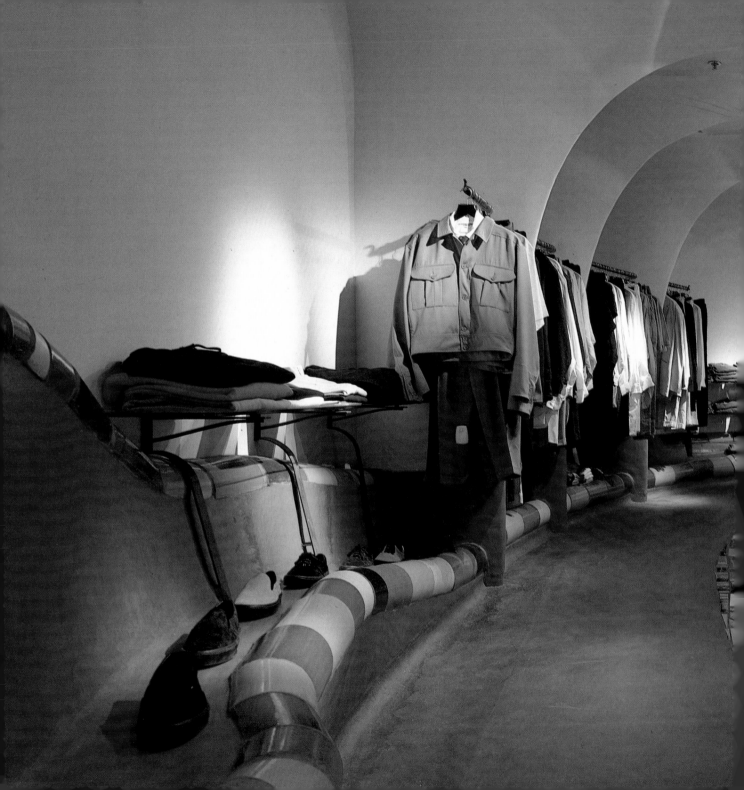

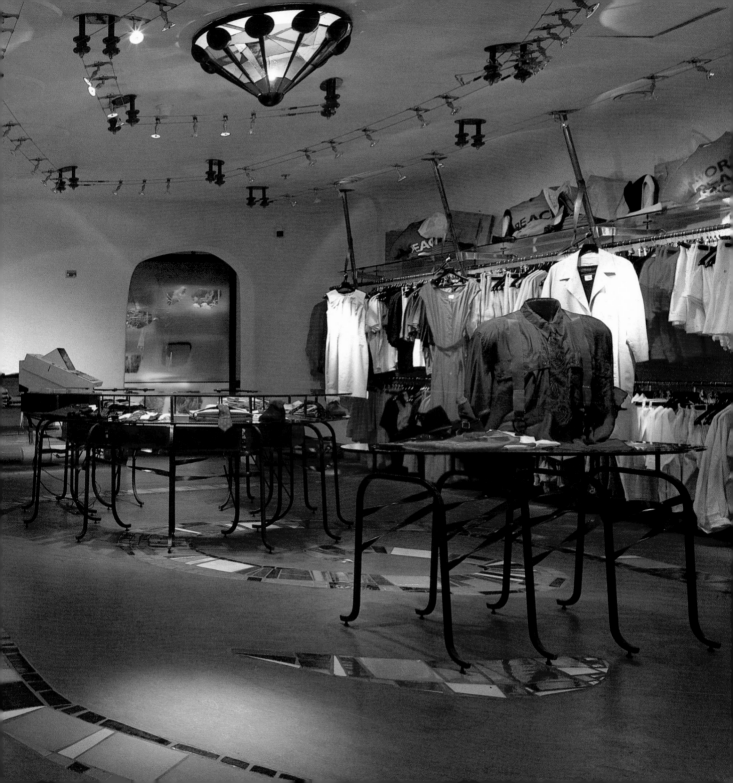

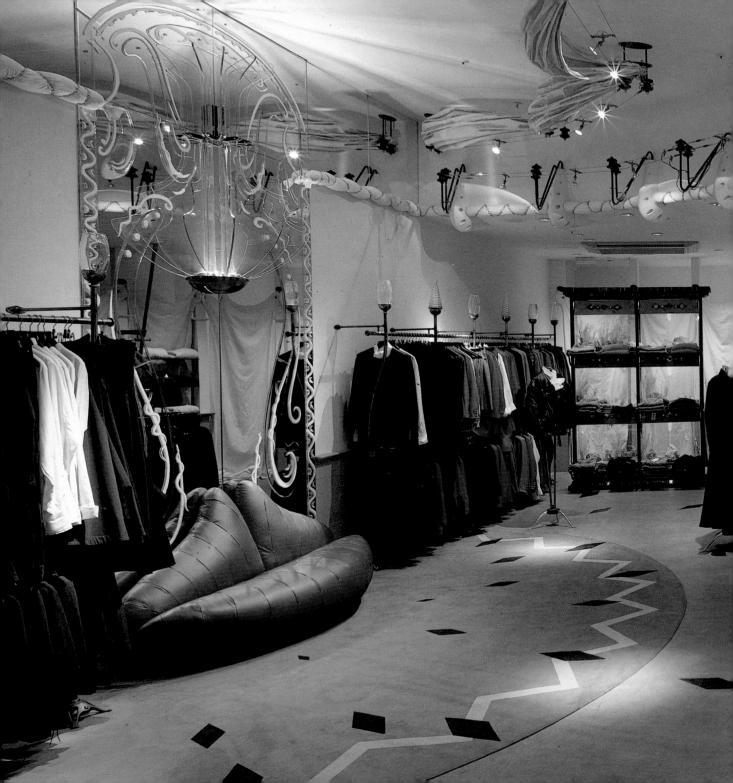

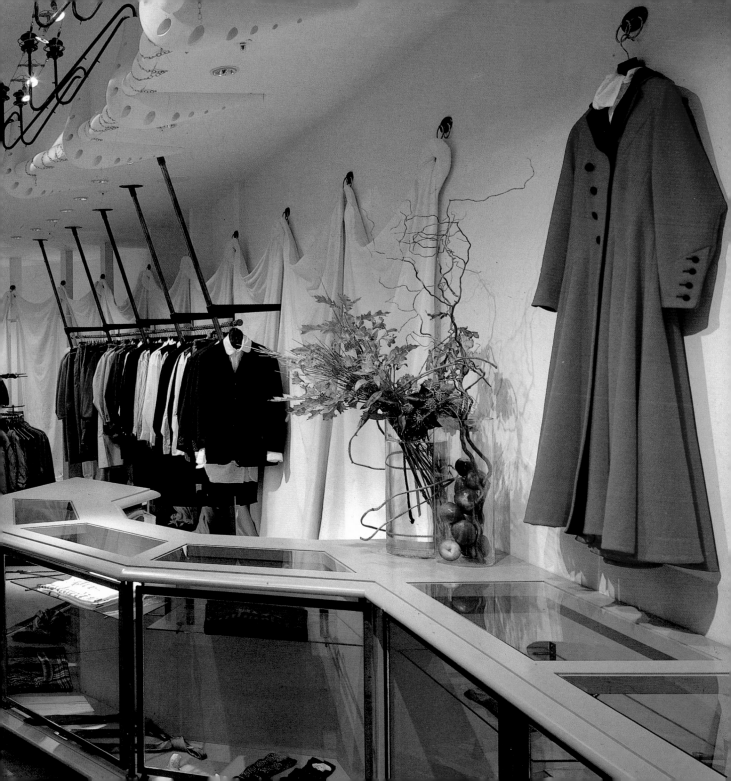

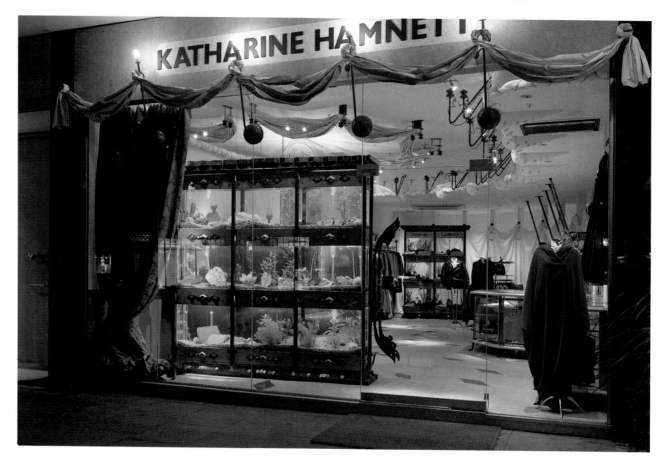

90

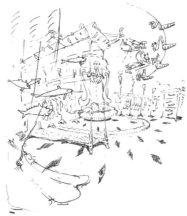

*Previous page, in
Hamnett's Sloane
Street shop a
counter and curved
ceiling deflect
visitors towards
the clothing rails.
The theatrical
shopfront, above,
is an invitation to
play the part of
"shopper". Right,
sketchbook
drawing*

*Jigsaw in High
Street Kensington
showed that some
of Coates's more
adventurous ideas
could be applied to
an ordinary chain
of fashion shops*

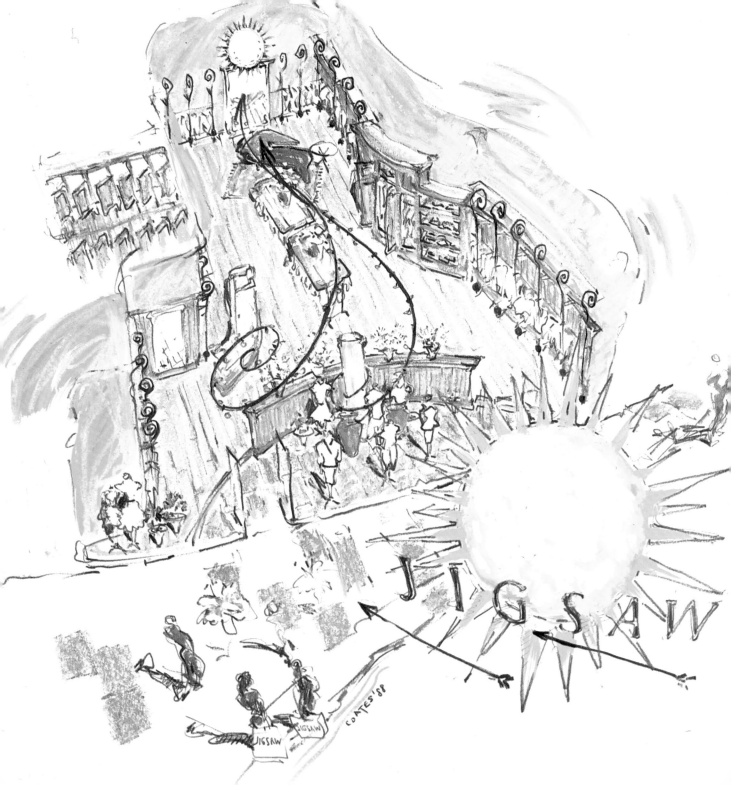

JIGSAW

COATES'88

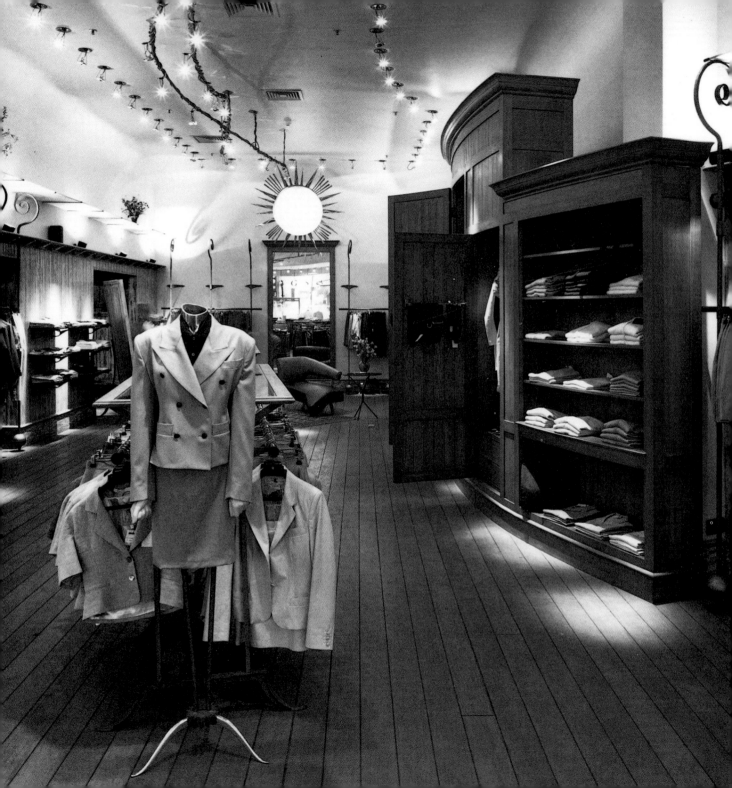

shop and they were also aware of the work in Japan. They were imaginative enough to see the potential for their own retail chain.

Many of the elements that Branson Coates brought to Jigsaw's flagship store, in a fashionable strip of High Street Kensington, are familiar from earlier projects. But the architects had more space to work with and the shop has a dynamism lacking in the smaller projects, which never achieve quite as much movement as the drawings lead you to expect. This is brought out most dramatically in the suspended lighting track, which curls round a column and twists down the length of the shop like a materialisation of one of the directional arrows in a Coates drawing. After several years in which high-street fashion shops have served up an unvarying diet of neat woodblock floors, matt black shelving units and discreet dichroic lamps, Jigsaw's sun-bleached, weatherboard aesthetic is genuinely fresh. The design has welcome elements of wit too: battered flagstones define a pre-shop area as though the pavement is breaking in from outside, the changing cubicles are like Victorian beach huts or stable doors and a Tom Dixon sun chandelier acts as a focal point at the end of the shop. Jigsaw shows that there is room for a much less rigidly programmatic approach to popular

design and suggests ways in which Coates and others might carry it through. He was even able to persuade the client to accept the idea of commissioning artists to contribute. Coates would certainly argue that retail projects these are a legitimate testing ground for ideas with much broader applications: "Shop design has undoubtedly become the first real territory for architecture to flex its muscles in the 'street' idiom, because shops do not pretend to solve the century's disillusion with architecture. Besides, the owner of a shop is usually more prepared to take risks than a bank looking for a new home in the City.... Any shop is a stage with the street as its audience. Somehow it must throw what is inside outwards to be caught by the passer-by; it must exploit and play with the building it is part of, yet simultaneously create a desire to be inside it. Shop design must transgress the division between interior and exterior; business depends on it."[8]

The question remains, though, of how such approaches might be transferred to the larger urban projects, which are where Coates's real ambitions lie.

93

Opposite, a twisting lighting track is used at Jigsaw to pull shoppers towards the Tom Dixon sun sculpture, right, at the end of the wedge-shaped space. Wood and stone finishes, far right, are rough and, for a high-street shop, experimental

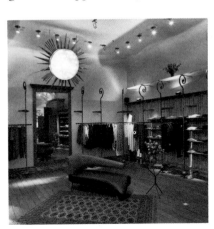
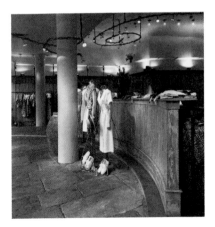

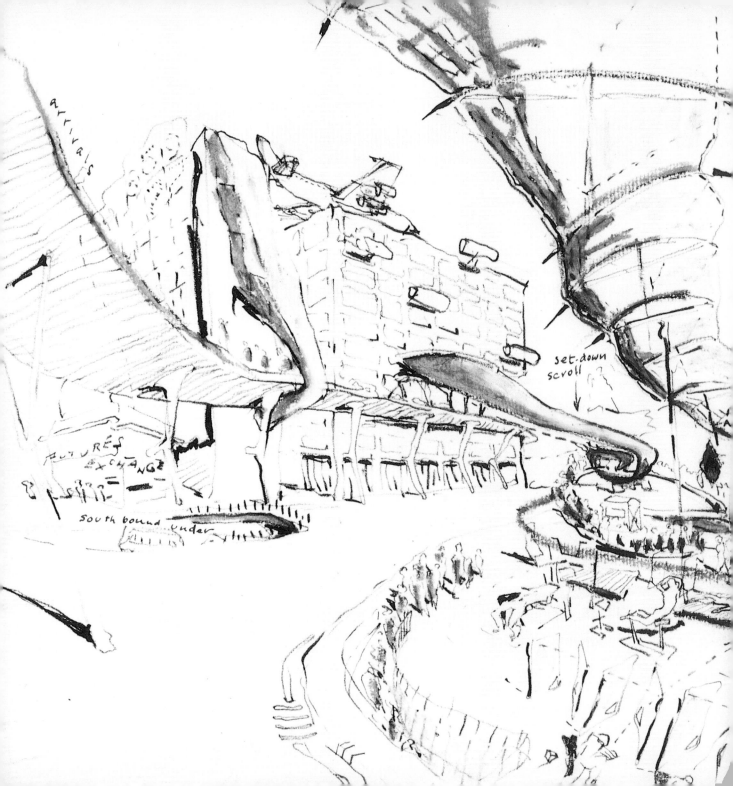

Chapter Five | Software City

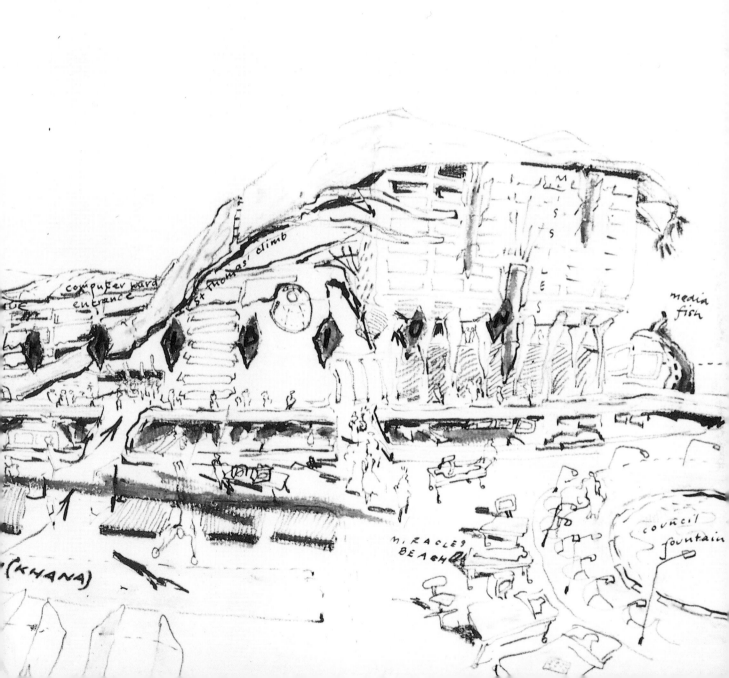

In 1935, Le Corbusier announced "the death of the street" in his plans for *La Ville Radieuse*. There would be no clogged and dirty thoroughfares, no teeming, foot-bound crowds, and little opportunity for chance encounter in this twentieth-century utopia. In the dawning age of the car, the populace would whisk between the zones of the radiant city using a network of super-efficient roadways. The city itself would be divided into areas for living, working and relaxing. Later, as promulgated in the *Athens Charter* of 1943, these principles became articles of modernist faith. Urban planners of the world have been applying them (many would say misapplying them) ever since.

But the street, of course, has refused to die, though it has often suffered at the planners' hands. Streets are the arteries and veins of the city in more than just a physical sense. For the people who use them, for all of us, they are alleyways of possibility, points of entry and departure, sites of encounter, transaction, discovery and display – a constantly unfolding drama in which the energies and tensions of the city are assembled and exposed. Often it seems that writers who deal with the culture of the city are more sensitive to this other life than the architects who design the buildings that line the streets. As the

critic Iain Chambers has noted: "The city exists as a series of doubles: it has official and hidden cultures, it is a real place and a site of the imagination. Its elaborate network of streets, housing, public buildings, transport systems, parks and shops is paralleled by a complex of attitudes, habits, customs, expectancies, and hopes that reside in us as urban subjects. We discover that urban 'reality' is not singular but multiple, that inside the city there is always another city.... Despite the intentions of architects and city planners to reduce the city to an abstract, rational order and geometrical purity, to a 'skeletal structure' (Mies van der Rohe), it remains a body redolent with the diverse richness and eroticism of the 'here and now'."[1]

For Jonathan Raban, writing in *Soft City*, "Living in cities is an art, and we need the vocabulary of art, of style, to describe the peculiar relationships between man and material that exists in the continual creative play of urban living. The city as we imagine it, the soft city of illusion, myth, aspiration, nightmare, is as real, maybe more real, than the hard city one can locate on maps in statistics, in monographs on urban sociology and demography and architecture."[2]

Chambers and Raban sound almost resigned to the separation between the two cities – but then they are not

96

architects. Should architecture be no more than a mute container, an impediment even, for this other life of the imagination? Coates is not the only architect in the 1980s to argue that architecture itself might take a more active role in Raban's "continual creative play of urban living". One of the most vital sources for his architecture, as we have seen, is the street. "Far from being another bland component of the city," he writes, "the street is its most essential and most ambiguous unit... an open framework for the drama of everyday living... the key dynamic model for the play between public and private, static and mobile, restraint and release."[3] And it is precisely "the vocabulary of art, of style" which Coates wants to apply to our buildings. Here he has a slightly improbable ally in the American sculptor-architect James Wines. With his organisation SITE, Wines has designed a series of notorious supermarkets for Best — one with a crumbling wall, another with a tilting storefront — which brought the scorn of the architectural establishment down on his head. In his book *De-Architecture* (1987), Wines takes the profession to task for its failure to produce buildings which either engage the public or say anything interesting about the society that created them. He contrasts architecture with the commentary offered by

painters, playwrights, film-makers and poets and finds it wanting on all counts. The formalism of the modernists, he claims, is "a vacuous game of elementary geometry" to everyone except architects because it refers only to itself.[4] Post-modernism's historical quotations are more decorative, but equally off-putting unless you are familiar with the references: "As an alternative, de-architecture suggests a rejection of Modernist role models, an expanded definition of architecture as a concept, and a use of buildings as a means of providing information and commentary rather than expressing form and symbol. The theory of de-architecture holds that throughout history the successful edifices, at their most intense level of communication, have been the product of psychological, social, cosmic, and metaphysical influences."[5]

Narrative architecture, Wines argues, is a way of reassembling the fragments created by de-architecture's demolition job on the prejudices we have about buildings. Old meanings are revealed in the process and new meanings arise from the rearrangement. But Wines's use of words such as "storyline" and "narration" (which Coates always avoids: narrative, for him, connotes motion not story) still suggests a more coherent, more literally

97

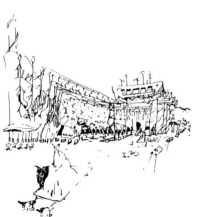

Right, section through Coates's entry for the Paris Opera competition (1983), his first attempt to apply narrative ideas to a real rather than theoretical project. Left, sketchbook detail of the front elevation

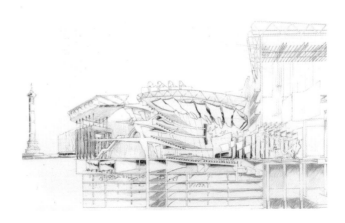

readable architecture than anything Coates has designed
so far, even if the narrative Wines envisages is delivered as
a series of fragmentary moments rather than as a
continuous whole. Indeed, Wines's entire programme,
his architecture and writing, has a clarity of intention
and expression that Coates sometimes lacks. It is not that
Coates is being wilfully obscure – more that the nature of
the sensations he wants his architecture to express is
harder to pin down. Where Wines's concerns are
sculptural, demanding a reappraisal of architecture's
status as sign, Coates's are spatial, committed to an
exploration of architecture's programmatic meaning. For
Coates, the use of imagery has as much to do with the
"staging" of space and the stage-direction of the user's
movements through the building as it does with content.
In this sense, Coates's work is closer to that of Frank
Gehry than it is to Wines's. At Rebecca's restaurant in
Venice, California, a project in many ways reminiscent of
Coates's interiors, Gehry employed superficially
outrageous "art" devices such as painted tin crocodiles, a
glass octopus and a row of tree-like timber columns as a
way of organising the bar and dining area and drawing
visitors through the space. In Gehry's work, as in
Coates's, objects are valued for their tactile qualities and
their power to act as lures for the senses.

It is the very intensity of his imagery, however, that
makes Coates's work, for some critics, so disturbing. For
writers who long for the contemplative restraint of the
modernist interior, projects such as the Caffè Bongo take
their place in a long line of clamorous, culture-denying
excesses that leads from the penny dreadful to the soap
opera and the video nasty: "Nigel Coates' interiors, like
so much of contemporary culture, seem to assume a
certain lack of interior life, or at least contact with a
constant self-sufficient identity. In the television era,
stimulus junkies with short attention spans want strident
distractions, not uncluttered space in which the soul may
surface and unfold."[6] What this doesn't allow, of course,
is the possibility that the hapless "stimulus junkie"
might bring anything of his own to the experience or take
anything away from it.

But Coates's ready embrace of our image-saturated
environment is controversial. In "The Ecstasy of
Communication" (1987), an essay that has become a
virtual scripture for media theorists and art critics the
world over, Jean Baudrillard announced that "We are no
longer a part of the drama of alienation; we live in an
ecstacy of communication. And this ecstasy is obscene."[7]

Baudrillard described the way in which our information-drenched media landscape, with its incessant demands on our attention and its reach into every cranny of our private space, has changed the very forms of perception and pleasure and caused interiority and intimacy to evaporate. For such an alarming notion, the language sounded strangely attractive, but Baudrillard went no further than asserting that he was not necessarily making a value judgement; we would have to put up with this new state of affairs. Coates, reading the essay, had no such reservations. He wrote that he preferred to take Baudrillard's observations on the advertising landscape and the disappearance of public space not as warnings, but as "points of departure". As for the "ecstasy of communication": "It is exactly this ecstasy which I applaud, if, that is, it can be freely experimented with by all of us. The role of architecture must be central, not because architecture is directly political, nor could it ever be, but because it is the duty of architecture to provide a usable laboratory with some decent equipment. The poverty of architecture has lasted long enough. This play with the erratic dimensions of perception is part of everybody's life – to the extent that our sense of space has changed fundamentally. Space, in the old architectural definition, relied on objects and how they looked. Space now synthesizes form, information and perception. It involves completely new rituals, like using VDUs and floppy discs. It relies on hidden information at every level."[8]

What Coates is proposing here is not simply a soft city but a software city. The architecture he envisages, and has begun to build, aspires to be an analogue to the hidden software processes and constant information transfer of the contemporary metropolis. He accepts, with his critics, that much of late twentieth-century life has been rendered banal, that "television is the new measure of our perceptions".[9] He acknowledges the coming of the "society of the spectacle" described by the Situationist Guy Debord, finding its most extreme manifestation in contemporary Japan where he himself has worked: "Japanese culture lacks the critical dimension of the West. It isn't a dialectical culture – it's a marketing culture. It's product-oriented and consumption-oriented in a way that a Situationist could never believe possible."[10]

One way of resisting the spectacle, Coates argues, is to take on its vocabulary, or the parts that interest us, and manipulate them to our own ends. In *Subculture: The*

99

Meaning of Style (1979), Dick Hebdige showed how subcultural groups, using a process of *bricolage* similar to that found among primitive peoples, appropriate the sacred artefacts or images of society (comb, suit and tie, Union Jack, swastika), recombine or redeploy them and invert their meanings.[11] Consumption might be inevitable, but that doesn't mean it has to be passive or follow the prescribed channels. Nor is Coates the first to suggest that the ad hoc methods of the *bricoleur* might be as relevant to the organisation of cities as the more logical approach of the scientist-planner. Colin Rowe and Fred Koetter made exactly this point in *Collage City* (1978), arguing with tortuous care that if a reconciliation of the two modes of thinking (the "savage" and the "civilised") were achieved, "it might even be possible to suppose that the way for a truly useful dialectic could be prepared".[12] Typically, Coates goes much further, advocating the use of the city's collage of existing monuments and delapidated buildings as a vital resource. The narrative architecture he proposes is open-ended, primed for take-over by its users. It sets out to create the conditions, the "richly stimulating chaos", in which creativity can occur. Embracing irrationality, procedural flexibility and caprice, city and building become fields of

"processes, interactions and symbols in balance", a kind of "symbolic software" assembled using techniques familiar from advertising and television (continuity, repetition, the shock and the cut).[13] Coates's completed projects suggest further ways in which such an architecture might combat the process of commodification: first, by including elements of critique to undermine their "credibility" (all of the Tokyo interiors, Silver and Katharine Hamnett, London); and second, by adopting a "performance"- and process-based approach which foregrounds the work of Coates's many artist collaborators (thirty-seven in number at the time of writing). The imperfect, layered, loose-fit feel that results from these interactions removes Coates's architecture from the realm of perfect object, product of a single masterful sensibility, and turns it into an aggregation of experiences that anticipates the life of the building to come. How much difference these strategies can make in the long run, given the limited, commercial nature of the projects' programmes, is an open question.

Coates himself dreams of building a public rather than private architecture. He believes, like James Wines in the US, that the expressive possibilities of such an architecture are greater than with painting or the other

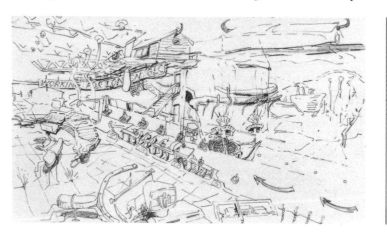

Coates's drawings of ArkAlbion, left and opposite, had the compulsive quality of automatic writing, but their intention was serious. Rejecting modernist planning, he proposed to combine factories, offices, shops and homes in one area

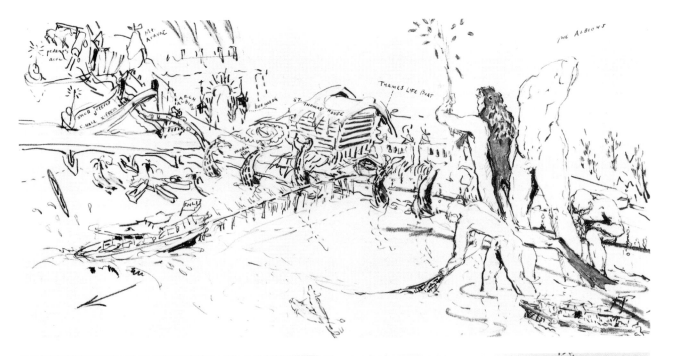

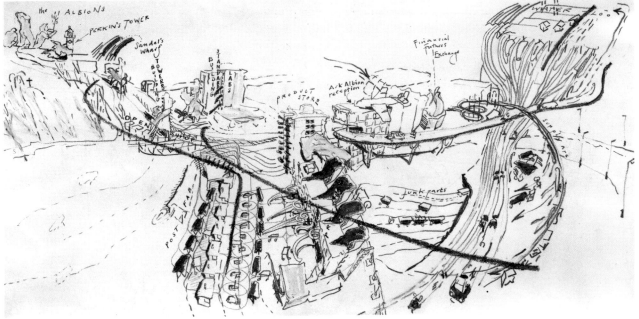

arts. Not everyone goes to art galleries, but buildings embrace all aspects of our lives; they accommodate people of all ages, backgrounds, outlooks and tastes. Many would see this as ample reason for architecture to proceed with restraint. By contrast, the buildings Coates proposes seem, on occasions, to aspire to a condition of near-hallucinogenic intensity. At the very least, he wants them to express pleasure and a sense of the moment in which they are created, to possess an "eroticism of the 'here and now'" (Chambers) that acknowledges the lives, desires and imagination of their users. In Coates's view, this will happen only when architects start to face up to the way that city life has changed. "Unless architecture as a form of culture embraces the nature of human events, it can't properly engage with the life that goes on in and around the building."[14] This concern with events is the theme that links Coates's researches of the 1970s to his activities with NATO and to his more recent projects. The plans of Coates's interiors and buildings are determined by his attempts to capture and encode their future uses and this is the standpoint, ultimately, from which all his work must be judged. One American magazine has accused him of "producing architecture to be photographed, and photographs to be architecture",

making a visit to any of the Tokyo projects unnecessary.[15] But Coates, like any architect, recognizes the distortions inherent in the photographic process even as he benefits from the publicity. The interiors derive from programmatic concerns, they exist in space and they are designed to generate physical experiences rather than pictorial ones. They can only be understood, in the end, by moving through them (this is not to say that they will always work).

Coates has been equally undeviating in his conviction that each of the districts in a city should encompass as many functions as possible – that a stimulating city is one in which people live where they work and take their recreation where they live. He is not alone in this. Other architects and urbanists in reaction against the precepts of the modern movement, such as Leon Krier, argue for much the same thing. But where Krier dreams of a pre-industrial artisan-paradise, which will paradoxically come about when the robots liberate us from toil, Coates is resolutely anti-utopian and prepared to work with the grain of the city rather than against it. "ArkAlbion", his exhibition at the Architectural Association in 1984, was a personal attempt to apply some of NATO's Albion ideas to London's County Hall and its neighbourhood. "In

Sketchbook map of ArkAlbion, plotting lines of movement and centres of activity, from the "software terraces" to the "art dock" behind County Hall

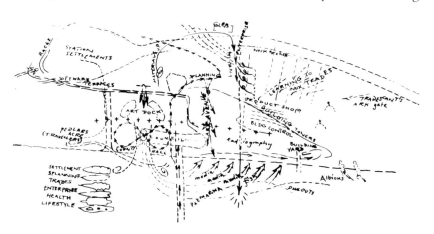

ArkAlbion, planning as we knew and hated it has gone, to be replaced by a much freer attitude to the way cities grow." Drawing on the example of the Festival of Britain, which had occupied the adjoining site, ArkAlbion was to function as a "living exhibition in which the public can witness the fusing of office, factory, shop [and] home into one volatile city fibre".[16] Where its buildings would differ from the festival's was in their commitment to multiple narratives rather than a single predictable storyline. In text, photographs and drawings, Coates overstated his case with his customary bravado and wit. ArkAlbion would offer short-stay cabins for travellers above the platforms at Waterloo Station, while long-term patients in St Thomas's hospital would use computer keyboards to devise slogans for the billboards outside. To encourage "more effective freestyling on the building sites", apprentices at the "City and Deguilds" school would learn not one but several trades. And so it went on: at all points, Coates's architectural proposals were indivisible from his idiosyncratic vision of new ways of living and working in the city.

There is an openness and a generosity to such a strategy that makes Coates rare among architects, but in the too serious world of architecture it is not always welcome. In an exhibition at London's Institute of Contemporary Arts in 1988, Coates put forward proposals for the area of land between two of the capital's great stations.[17] Eurofields, as he called it, would celebrate the dismantling of European trade barriers in 1992. "Kings Cross and St Pancras have a curious gap between them – why not have a blistering electronic countryside oozing out, like jam out of a sandwich? As the gap between the two platform sheds widens, trees and the neons poking through them cut through a new shopping Broadway based on two of our Japanese buildings, Nishiazabu and Ashiya. Here European stores like Karstaat, De Bijenkorf, Aux Printemps (sic) and Upim mix with company embassies and red light bars in Cappadocian cones."[18] What visitors to the exhibition saw was a vast model of the site, held together by motorway crash barriers. The "embassies" were made from ceramic electric fire components; pulsating rubber gear-stick casings stood in for butter mountains; and plasticine, pegboard, radio valves, windscreen wiper motors and a train-set all played a part. There would be a duty-free Harrods, a "sin centre", trade halls, service halls, kasbahs and a wine lake all packed into one decomposed and recomposed site. Five video screens, two turned on their side, "explained"

103

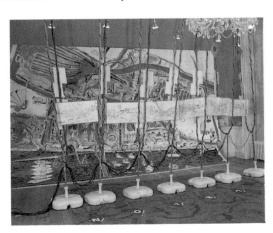

Right, the ArkAlbion installation at the Architectural Association in 1984. The floor was a painted stand-in for the River Thames and the model, in NATO fashion, was a pile of junk

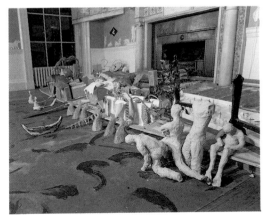

the project in disembodied android voices. Coates himself was rather easier to understand and his message was by now familiar: "The city is a continuous space in which one event should lead to the next with the occasional eye-catching incident. The notion that architecture should build walls – the concept behind zoning regulations – is something I'm against. Each part of the city should do two or three things."[19]

In Eurofields, Coates showed how the preoccupations of NATO might be filtered through the discoveries of his built work to produce an architecture that was soft and naturalistic in appearance rather than hard-edged and technological. Eurofields was hardly intended to be read as a blueprint, but it did suggest strategies for dealing as sympathetically as possible with the undeveloped landscape of the city as a living entity. It challenged the notion that the modern office has to mean vast and undifferentiated areas of serviced space in characterless boxes by treating the entire area as a kind of "nature trail", a monument to the countryside in the same way that St Pancras is a monument to Victorian travel. In Coates's drawing, the architectural forms have the extruded, overlapping quality of musculature, binding the existing buildings of the site, the natural features of

the landscape and his own additions into an organic and evolutionary whole whose starting point, as in all Coates's work, is the body. The exhibition might not have addressed the issues of "land tenure, habitation, transportation and information technology", as one editorial lamented in the tones of a stern parent correcting a wayward child.[20] But where Eurofields was concerned that was hardly the point. The project had a sense of optimism, energy and warped good humour that no amount of disengaged infrastructural planning could by itself supply. It offered a vision of London as workspace and pleasure centre that was completely at odds with the inward-looking corporate architecture going up in the City. It was a tongue-in-cheek corrective that suggested, to a capital in danger of forgetting, that architecture has a duty to engage with the present for the benefit of us all. In this, more than in any passing consideration of style, fashion or even content, lies the importance and the potential of Coates's work.

104

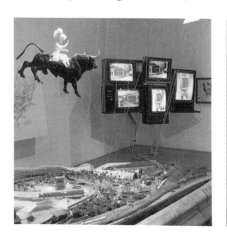

For the "Metropolis" exhibition at London's ICA, Branson Coates's unorthodox model-making skills were brought to bear on the undeveloped land between Kings Cross and St Pancras stations

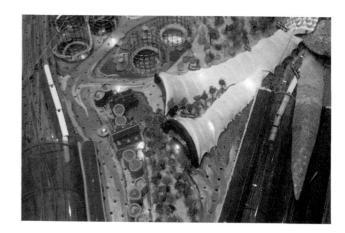

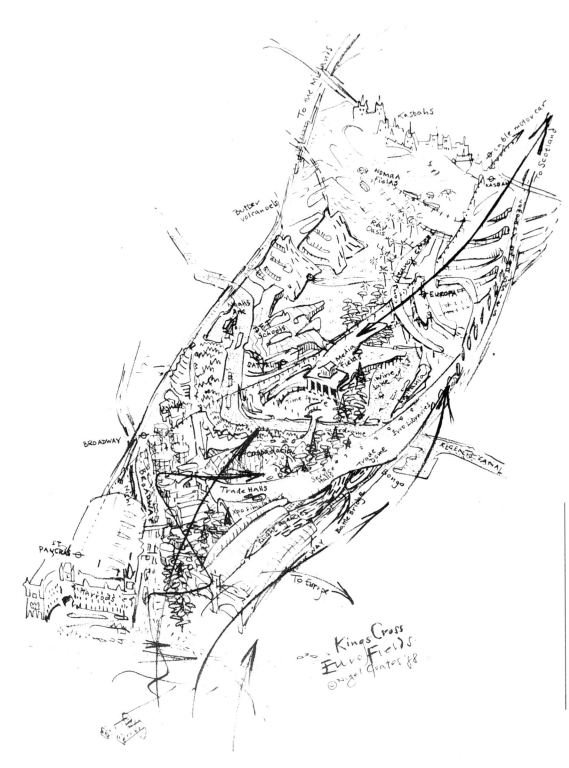

The labels visible in the drawing include: To the Midlands, Kasbahs, cable motorcar, To Scotland, Butter volcanoes, NOMAD fields, RAIN OASIS, Kasbahs, Noahs Ark, EUROPA, Schools, SATELLITE, Media Fields, Wine Lake, Euro Libraries, BROADWAY, Time Square, Geodome, COMMODORE, Trade Halls, Service Halls, Trade Dome, Bongo, Xpo Finali..., REGENTS CANAL, ST PANCRAS, Harrods, Babe Bridge, To Europe, Kings Cross EuroFields © Nigel Coates '88

105

Coates's drawing of the Eurofields proposal shows the landscape of the new city erupting in the gap between the stations. Work and leisure functions combine in a vision of London as a multi-layered playground

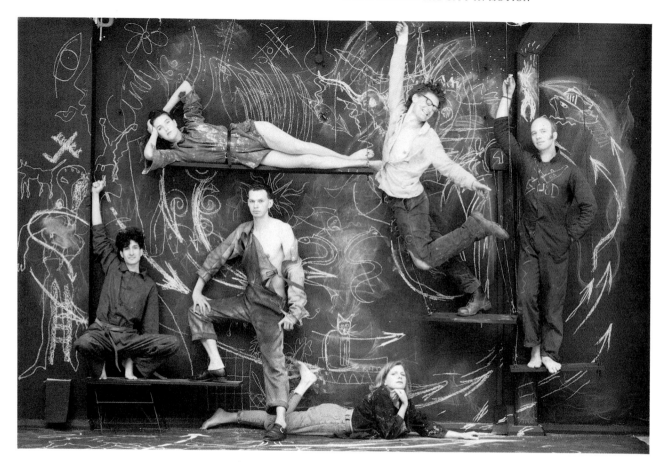

Coates, right, and some of his artist collaborators. From left to right, Carlos Villanueva Brandt, Zaza Wentworth Stanley, Tom Dixon, Annabel Grey and Mark Prizeman

Notes

Introduction

1 N. Coates, "The City in Motion", in *Metropolis: New British Architecture and the City*, The Institute of Contemporary Arts, London, 1988.
2 D. Dietsch, "The Empire strikes Back", *Architectural Record*, September 1987, pp. 142–143.
3 See in particular: J. McClellan and S. Beard, "Blueprints on the East", *Arena*, No 10, July/August 1988, pp.130–135; L. Jobey, "Signs of the Times", *Vogue*, November 1988, pp. 198–201, 283.
4 J. Wines, "The Slippery Floor", *Stroll*, No 6/7, June 1988, pp. 15–23.
5 C. Jencks, "The New Expressionism", in *Architecture Today*, Academy Editions, London, 1988, pp. 222–229. According to Jencks, other practitioners of this approach, which began in the late 1970s in parallel with similar developments in the art world, include Günther Domenig, Peter Cook and Christine Hawley, and Frank Gehry.
6 "Leading Edge", Axis Gallery, Tokyo, December 1988. Exhibitors included Daniel Weil, Geoff Hollington, Shiu Kay Kan and Paul Priestman.
7 Most obviously they include Tom Dixon, André Dubreuil, Oriel Harwood and members of the NATO group. For background on these developments in British design in the 1980s, see: J. Thackara, ed., *New British Design*, Thames and Hudson, London, 1986; C. McDermott, *Street Style: British Design in the 80s*, Design Council, London, 1987.
8 Compare, for instance, E. Farrelly, "NATO: Well-bred Street Cred", *The Architectural Review*, Vol CLXXIX No 1069, March 1986, pp. 75–77 and P. Smith, "Terminal Culture? 'The British Edge'", *Art in America*, September 1987, pp. 36–39, 41.
9 S. Sontag, "Notes on 'Camp'", in *Against Interpretation*, Dell Publishing Co, New York, 1978, pp. 275–292 (originally published in *Partisan Review*, 1964).
10 See G. Crysler, "Architectural Dandyism in the Age of Mass Media", *New Art Examiner*, Vol 16 No 11, Summer 1989, pp. 32–34.
11 S. Sontag, "Notes on 'Camp'", p. 289.

Chapter One: Diploma Unit 10

1 H. Lefebvre, *Everyday Life in the Modern World*, trans., Harper Torchbooks, New York, 1971 (originally published as *La vie quotidienne dans le monde moderne*, Editions Gallimard, Paris, 1968).
2 *Ibid.*, p. 205.
3 B. Tschumi, *Chronicle in Urban Politics*, Architectural Association, London, 1974. See also B. Tschumi, *Chronicle of Space*, Architectural Association, London, 1975.
4 Interview with the author, January 1989.
5 See "Millbank Competition: Reflections on the State of British Architecture", *Architectural Design*, Vol XLVII No 7/8, July/August 1977, p. 519.
6 Interview with the author, January 1989.
7 N. Coates, "Narrative Break-up", in *The Discourse of Events*, Themes 3, Architectural Association, London, 1983, pp. 12–17.
8 N. Coates, "Modern Life and the Impact of Architecture", Diploma Unit 10, *Projects Review 1980–81*, Architectural Association, London, 1981.
9 *Ibid.*
10 N. Coates, "New Clubs at Large", *AA Files*, No 1, Autumn 1981, pp. 4–8.
11 N. Coates, "Ski Station", *ArkAlbion and Six Other Projects*, Architectural Association, London, 1984, pp. 42–43.

Chapter Two: NATO Manoeuvres

1 Quoted in N. Coates, "Ghetto & Globe", *AA Files*, No 5, Spring 1984, pp. 60–68.
2 *NATO*, No 1, Architectural Association, London, 1983.
3 See P. York, "Style Wars", *AA Files*, No 1, Autumn 1981, pp. 25–28 and *Style Wars*, Sidgwick and Jackson, London, 1980.
4 C. Norton, "The Fabric Factory", in *The Discourse of Events*, Themes 3, Architectural Association, London, 1983, pp. 88–89.
5 A. Sant'Elia, "Manifesto of Futurist Architecture 1914", in U. Apollonio, ed., *Futurist Manifestos*,

Thames and Hudson, London, 1973, p. 170.

6 N. Coates, "Giant Sized Baby Town", Diploma Unit 10, *Projects Review 1981–82*, Architectural Association, London, 1982.

7 N. Coates, "Ghetto & Globe", p. 62.

8 Quoted in D. Kirkpatrick, *Eduardo Paolozzi*, Studio Vista, London, 1970, p. 122.

9 P. Fleissig, "Do Walls have Ears?", *NATO*, No 1, pp. 4–5.

10 N. Coates, "Ghetto & Globe", p. 64.

11 *Ibid*.

12 See N. Coates, *ArkAlbion and Six Other Projects*, Architectural Association, London, 1984.

13 N. Coates, "Gamma-start", *NATO*, No 3, Gamma-City issue, Architectural Association, London, 1985, p. 13.

14 *Ibid*.

15 Quoted in B. Hatton, "Produkti for Metamorpolis", *AA Files*, No 12, Summer 1986, pp. 102–106.

16 I. Blazwick, "Pop Life", *NATO*, No 3, p. 11.

17 Interview with the author, March 1989.

18 Hatton, *op. cit.*, p. 106.

19 J. Lubbock, "AA Unit 10: Surreal Sources", *The Architects' Journal*, 12 October 1983, pp. 97–99.

20 P. Dormer, "These Dog Turd Days", *The Face*, No 79, November 1986, pp. 104, 107.

21 S. Sontag, *On Photography*, Penguin Books, Harmondsworth, 1979, pp. 68–69.

22 Quoted in B. Hatton, "Combined Operations", *Building Design*, 17 July 1987, pp. 16–17.

23 NATO in *The British Edge*, The Institute of Contemporary Art, Boston, 1987, p. 22.

Chapter Three: Tokyo Non-stop

1 D. Hebdige, "Digging for Britain: an Excavation in 7 Parts", in *The British Edge*, The Institute of Contemporary Art, Boston, 1987, p. 55.

2 Quoted in C. McDermott, "Anarchic Architect", *Creative Review*, Vol 6 No 4, April 1986, pp. 59, 61.

3 N. Coates, "Branson Coates: the Metropole Restaurant and Current Work", *AA Files*, No 12, Summer 1986, pp. 19–20.

4 Figure quoted in G. Vorreiter, "Japan", *The Architectural Review*, Vol CLXXXII No 1089, November 1987, special issue on Japan, pp. 38–43.

5 Quoted in J. Thackara, "Seeing is Disbelieving", *The Listener*, 23 March 1989, pp. 35–37.

6 Quoted in J. McClellan and S. Beard, "Blueprints on the East", *Arena*, No 10, July/August 1988, pp. 130–135.

7 Quoted in L. Grossman, "The Marquis de Facade", *Harpers & Queen*, March 1987, pp. 164–165.

8 N. Coates and the NATO group, "NATO's Fast Forward: Tokyo 1997", *Brutus*, No 157, April 1987, p. 42.

9 *Ibid*.

10 Interview with the author, July 1989.

11 *Ibid*.

12 N. Coates, undated message to CIA, Tokyo. Coates's handwriting was blown up to billboard proportions.

13 Interview with the author, July 1989.

14 See C. Jencks, *Bizarre Architecture*, Academy Editions, London, 1979.

Chapter Four: Industrial Baroque

1 N. Coates, "Branson Coates: the Metropole Restaurant and Current Work", *AA Files*, No 12, Summer 1986, pp. 19–20.

2 S. Calloway, *Designs for Interiors*, Victoria and Albert Museum, 1986, p. 28.

3 Quoted in L. Grossman, "The Marquis de Facade", *Harpers & Queen*, March 1987, pp. 164–165.

4 Interview with the author, June 1987.

5 Quoted in I. Crawford, "Silver", *The World of Interiors*, September 1987, pp. 136–143.

6 Quoted in M. Pawley, "Curiosity Shop", *The Guardian*, 28 November 1988, p. 38.

7 Interview with the author, July 1989.

8 N. Coates, "Street Signs", in J. Thackara, ed., *Design After Modernism: Beyond the Object*, Thames and Hudson, London, 1988, pp. 95–114.

Chapter Five: Software City

1 I. Chambers, *Popular Culture: The Metropolitan Experience*, Methuen, London and New York, 1986, p. 183.

2 J. Raban, *Soft City*, Collins Harvill, London, 1988, p. 10 (originally published in 1974).

3 N. Coates, "Street Signs", in J. Thackara, ed., *Design After Modernism: Beyond the Object*, Thames and Hudson, London, 1988, p. 107.

4 J. Wines, *De-Architecture*, Rizzoli International, New York, 1987, p. 118.

5 *Ibid*., p. 33.

6 P. Buchanan, "The Nostalgic Now: Flyte, Fellini and Ferlinghetti", *The Architectural Review*, Vol CLXXXIII No 1091, January 1988, pp. 66, 70.

7 J. Baudrillard, "The Ecstasy of Communication" in H. Foster, ed., *Postmodern Culture*, Pluto Press, London, 1985, pp. 126–134.

8 N. Coates, "Street Signs", pp. 112–113.

9 *Ibid*., p. 78.

10 Interview with the author, February 1989.

11 D. Hebdige, *Subculture: The Meaning of Style*, Methuen, London, 1979.

12 C. Rowe and F. Koetter, *Collage City*, MIT Press, Cambridge, Massachusetts and London, 1983, p. 105 (original hardback edition 1978).

13 Three preceding quotations from N. Coates, "Street Signs".

14 Interview with the author, July 1989.

15 G. Crysler, "Architectural Dandyism in the Age of Mass Media", *New Art Examiner*, Vol 16 No 11, Summer 1989, pp. 32–34.

16 Two preceding quotations from N. Coates, *ArkAlbion and Six other Projects*, Architectural Association, London, 1984, p. 11.

17 "Metropolis", Institute of Contemporary Arts, London, August–October 1988. Ron Arad, Zaha Hadid, Future Systems, Daniel Weil and Gerard Taylor, and John Pawson and Claudio Silvestrin were also participants.

18 N. Coates, "The City in Motion", in *Metropolis: New British Architecture and the City*, The Institute of Contemporary Arts, London, 1988.

19 Quoted in J. Abrams, "Jeux sans Frontières", *The Independent*, 5 August 1988, p. 18.

20 "Reality and Nightmare", *The Architects' Journal*, 17 August 1988, p. 5.

Selected Bibliography

Archigram *Archigram*, Studio Vista, London, 1972

Bandini, M. "Ark de Triomphe", *Building Design*, 26 October 1984

Buchanan, P. "Bernard Tschumi, Nigel Coates", *The Architectural Review*, Vol CLXXIV No 1040, October 1983, special issue on the Architectural Association

Coates, N. "L'Art, Le Sphinx", *Artscribe*, No 3, Summer 1976

"Between the Axes: The Theatrical Garden", *Harpers & Queen*, April 1981

"Big Bofill and the Architect's Disguise", *Harpers & Queen*, February 1981

"Cook's Chefs-d'oeuvre", *The Architectural Review*, Vol CLXXV No 1045, March 1984

"Forward to the Drawing-Board", *Harpers & Queen*, January 1982

"Iron Curtain goes Up", *Blueprint*, No 46, April 1988

"Metropole Restaurant, Tokyo", *Architecture and Urbanism*, No 185, February 1986

"Nightlives of the Artists", in *Architettura 'corretta'*, Casa del Mantegna, Mantova, Italy, 1981 (exhibition catalogue)

Projects Review, Diploma Unit 10, Architectural Association, London: "Modern Life and the Impact of Architecture", 1981; "Giant Sized Baby Town", 1982; "Albion", 1983; "Voxhall", 1984; "Trading Spaces", 1985

A Space: A Thousand Words, Dieci Libri, Italy, 1975 (exhibition catalogue)

"Spiculations for Tomorrow", *Harpers & Queen*, January 1981

"Tokyo Tendenze", *Per Lui*, No 39, June 1986

"3 Architetti in Barca", *Modo*, May 1983

Chen, S. "Tokyo Transformer: CIA's 'Driving Force'", *Telescope*, No 2, September/October/November 1988, interview

Cook, P. "Strange Pavilions of the Mind", *AA Files*, No 4, Autumn 1983

Dannatt, A. "Retreats of Fashion", *The Architectural Review*, Vol CLXXXV No 1103, January 1989

Dormer, P. "Nigel and the Others", *Blueprint*, No 22, November 1985

Hatton, B. "A Collide-oscope, or Real Allegory", *AA Files*, No 9, Summer 1985

"Configuring Mercurius: Code to Capriccio", in N. Coates, *ArkAlbion and Six other Projects*, Architectural Association, 1984

"Industrial Capriccio", *Artscribe*, No 56, February/March 1986

"NATO's Building Regs", *NATO*, No 3, Architectural Association, London, 1985

"Personnel Files", *Building Design*, 11 April 1986

"Radical Dilettantes and Bookworms", *Building Design*, 24 February 1984

"Who is Sylvia? What is NATO?", *ZG*, No 13, Spring 1985

Manser, J. "Nigel's Fishing Trip", *Designers' Journal*, No 43, January 1989

de Moubray, A. "I'm Nigel, Fly Me", *The Architects' Journal*, 24 April 1985

Okagawa, M. "Restaurant, Tokyo", *The Architectural Review*, Vol CLXXIX No 1072, June 1986

Popham, P. "Big in Japan", *Blueprint*, No 53, December/January 1989

"Foreign Legion", *Blueprint*, No 34, February 1987

"Japan: Superpatron of Daring Design", *Metropolitan Home*, December 1988

Tokyo: The City at the End of the World, Kodansha International, Tokyo, 1985

Poynor, R. "Coates rebuilds the Ark in Japan", *Blueprint*, No 44, February 1988

"Nigel Coates: NATO Exercises", *Designers' Journal*, No 29, September 1987

Takiguchi, N. "Nigel Coates' Creative Network", *Axis*, Vol 32, Summer 1989

Thackara, J. "Mad Methods", *NATO*, No 3, Architectural Association, London, 1985

Tresidder, M. "Nigel Furioso", *The World of Interiors*, June 1988

Tschumi, B. "Spaces and Events", in *The Discourse of Events*, Themes 3, Architectural Association, London, 1983

York, P. "Pasolini meets Palladio", *Harpers & Queen*, October 1980

Projects

1985
Jasper Conran house, London
Metropole restaurant, Tokyo
*Artists: Edward Allington, Tom Dixon, Andrew
James, Adam Lowe, João Penalva, Valerie
Robertson, Michael Scott, Zaza Wentworth Stanley*

1986
Caffè Bongo, Parco department store, Tokyo
*Artists: Jasper Conran, Ron O'Donnell, André
Dubreuil, Adam Lowe, David Phillips, Zaza
Wentworth Stanley*
Bohemia jazz club, Takeo Kikuchi building, Tokyo
*Artists: Catrina Beevor, Judy Levy, Bruce McLean,
Mark Prizeman, Peter Sabara, Peter Thomas*
Takeo Kikuchi shop, Takeo Kikuchi building,
Tokyo
*Artists: Tom Dixon, André Dubreuil, John Keane,
Adam Lowe, Carlos Villanueva Brandt, Nick
Welch, Robert Mull*
Barber's shop, Takeo Kikuchi building, Tokyo
Jasper Conran shop, London

1987
Silver jewellery shop, London
Artists: Tom Dixon, André Dubreuil
Ashiya Pavilion commercial building, Ashiya,
Japan (unbuilt)
Jasper Conran shop, Dublin
Furniture collection for Rockstone, Tokyo

1988
Dunhill International exhibition, Mall Galleries,
London; Simpson's department store, Toronto
Artist: Tom Dixon
Katharine Hamnett shop, Glasgow
Artist: Marianne Dixon
Katharine Hamnett shop, London
Artists: Tom Dixon, Zaza Wentworth Stanley
Jigsaw shop, London
Artists: Tom Dixon, André Dubreuil
Jigsaw shop, Bristol
Artist: Mark Brazier-Jones
L'Arca di Noè restaurant building, Sapporo
*Artists: Beverly Beeland, Tom Dixon, Annabel
Grey, Oriel Harwood, Stuart Helm, Adam Lowe,
Jasper Morrison, Marc Quinn*
Noah furniture collection for SCP, London

1989
Jasper Conran shop, Seibu department store, Tokyo
Stonehenge shop, Stonehenge, Salisbury
Artist: Will Wentworth Stanley
Situationist International exhibition, Centre
George Pompidou, Paris; Institute of
Contemporary Arts, London; Institute of
Contemporary Art, Boston
Artists: Why Not Associates
Hotel Otaru Marittimo, Otaru, Japan
*Artists: Beverly Beeland, Mark Brazier-Jones, Tom
Dixon, Dirk van Dooren, Annabel Grey, Emma*

*Harrison, Oriel Harwood, Stuart Helm, Steve
Husband, Andrew James, Wilma Johnson, Kate
Malone, Simon Moore, Toby Roche, Karen
Spurgin, Zaza Wentworth Stanley, Why Not
Associates*

1990
The Wall, Nishi Azabu, Tokyo
Artists: Tom Dixon, Grayson Perry, Jessica Thomas

Architects and staff 1984–89
Tom Alexander, Fereshteh Apicella, Allan Bell,
Anne Brooks, Stephanie Caridis, Dominique
Cullinen, Gerrard O'Carroll, Mike Delaney, Simon
Eagar, Christophe Egret, Bosco Fair, Innes
Ferguson, Liz Gardner, Ayala Gill, Chris Haine,
Ross Logie, Jane McAllister, Frazer McKim, Louisa
Millar, Allan Mitchell, David Naessens, Bobbie
Oliver, Stuart Parr, Marta Pedrosa, Jeremy Pitts,
Rebecca du Pont, Oriel Prizeman, Luca Ridone,
Peter Sabara, Vijay Taheem, Peter Thomas, Cathi
du Toit, Oonagh Toner, Mike Tonkin, Carlos
Villanueva Brandt

Index

111